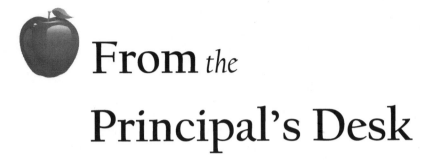

From *the*
Principal's Desk

21 Lessons in Passionpreneurship

STEFANI MCDADE MORROW

From the Principal's Desk
Copyright © 2014 by Stefani McDade Morrow

ISBN-10:0990991105
ISBN-13:978-0-9909911-0-6

Printed in the United States of America
First Edition 2015

Library of Congress Control Number: 2015901226

Published by
Villa Morrow Empowerment Group
P.O. Box 1581
Midlothian, Texas 76065
www.villamorrow.com

Edited by Michelle Matthews Calloway, PhD
Author Photo by Glam Unlimited Design Studio
Cover Design by Moze Print and Design

Praise from readers of

From *the* Principal's Desk

"Stefani has a wonderful way of connecting with the spirit of her readers. You'll quickly realize you have the power to break out of the status quo and unleash the passionpreneurship inside of you!"

   -Monica Lynne Foster, author of Today is Your Last Day...Say Wh?! and Founder of Women Who Run Their World

"I am often asked to mentor young entrepreneurs. When I do, I have a recommended list of books that I deem as must- read material to help prepare the young entrepreneur on their journey to success. This book is now at the top of that list."

   -Kaye Flewellen, The Hair Maven and author of Mane Attraction

"After reading *From the Principal's Desk*, I know I am single-handedly responsible for my OWN success. I am more confident and equipped to take this journey toward my passion. This is a quick read and provided life lessons on how to push toward your dream. It is a must read if you are ready to change your life and enter into your passion."

   -Shante' J. McCoy, McShell Educational Consulting

"There comes a time in life when one should ask the question, "What have I been created to do?" If you are at this juncture, Stefani's book will offer easy-to-learn lessons that will help you transition from mediocrity to success. With transition, work is required and this book will help you get the work done."

-Larry Kines, Single-Parent Empowerment Coach

"There are many books that challenge and change. This book speaks to the longing and passion in the reader to be greater. That greatness will in turn allow the real *you* to soar."
-LaDonya Adger, Creationeers Designs

"This book frees you to live your best life with intention. She takes you on a journey that outlines the steps you'll need to take to reach your next level."
-Carma Morgan, Owner & CEO of Carma Couture

"*From the Principal's Desk* exudes power and encourages the reader to invest in their success. It drives home the point of life-long learning and seeking out your destiny in an effort to leave your mark in the world."
-LaKeiah Cheatham, Co-Founder of Ring Leaders Marriage Group

"The pages in this book will fan the flame of courage in readers and help them in determining their *why*, or if they even have a *why*."
-Pamela McDade, The Counseling Diva

"It's hard to believe this book is Stefani's first! The content is rich and written in a way that will penetrate the hearts and pierce the thinking of readers. Many in life are at an impasse and looking for a prototype to create a more fulfilled existence. *From the Principal's Desk* is that guide."
-Gene A. Morrow, Co-Founder of Villa Morrow Empowerment Group

"This book is filled with joy, hope and promise! Through this quick and powerful read, Stefani reminds us that we are single-handedly responsible for our destiny and we can all be on a journey filled with greatness if we first envision it and put in the hard work to make it so."

-Leah Martisko Copeland, Ph.D., School Principal

"Stefani does a fantastic job helping the reader to focus on the tools that shape the framework for a growth mindset."

-Schretta Stewart-Mays, Academic Advisor

"There were pages where I lingered and lessons I reread. The words resonated in my soul page after page. I found myself frequently stopping to give my brain time to embrace the wisdom on the page while anticipating the next nugget."

-Cheryl Rischer, Founder of Mocha MOB (Mommy of Boys)

"This is a book I will read over and over again. It helps and encourages the reader to understand fully the power of our words and how the words we speak are either adding to us or robbing us."

-Donnya Christopher, Owner of Exquisite Designs

"In this book Stefani offers a series of practical lessons aimed at helping one to better themselves personally and professionally. With the lesson-centered approach readers will find it easy to be energized and find the initiative needed to realize their dreams and ambitions."

-Monique Rogers, Educator and Author of Cupcakes, Candles and Cancer

"This book exceeded my expectations. It challenges you to look at your strengths and develop your gifts while moving towards your passion and life's calling. It reminds you that YOU are in control of your own destiny."

-Tony Crawford, Founder of Big Hearts ATL

"I found *From the Principal's Desk* to be inspiring, thought-provoking and uplifting. Stefani does an excellent job sharing her journey to passionpreneurship while also inviting the reader to join the ride. Throughout the book her message is clear-pursue your passions and dreams to the fullest."

-Christi Bell, Educator and Entrepreneur

"There are books that raise the standard and there are books that set the standard. *From the Principal's Desk* would be the latter. I personally had many self-realization moments and began to examine my own life and ask myself the hard questions while reading. It was as if she was talking directly to me and where I am in life. My personal takeaway was to nominate myself for greatness."

-Demitri Sargent, Holistic Health & Wellness Coach

"This book reveals real-life challenges and principles that apply to all, regardless of status or pay grade. Stefani allows the reader to be a part of her journey, and in doing so forces them to question their life's goals. This work is one that will encourage you to recalibrate your thinking about leaving a legacy."

-Torey Page, Educational Consultant

Dedication

This book is dedicated to people searching for the courage to expect, create and experience a more fulfilled existence.

Acknowledgements

To Gene, my husband and friend, business partner, coach and very best father any child could ever have. Your support of this vision has been priceless and has never gone unnoticed. Together, we win or we perish! To my children, Madison and Mason, your love for me makes me smile. The two of you are my greatest work! To my mother, who helped me with my family while I was married to my manuscript, thanks a million. To my sisters and extended family, thanks for your support. To TS, we are the epitome of BFF! To my Gathering of the Giraffes network and personal master mind group, your belief in me is at times inconceivable. Your unwavering support produced the energy and confidence needed to write this book. Lastly, to a man whom I've never met in person, but whose teachings have single-handedly elevated my thinking to the next level, Mr. Les Brown. My ear was appointed to your voice at a time when I needed inspiration and direction at a very pivotal stage in my life. Thanks to you all and know our best days are yet ahead of us!

Table of Contents

Introduction

Instead of having a lavish Sweet 16 celebration, I started working at Grandy's Chicken on my 16th birthday. It was my official entrance to the work force and I was elated. The youngest of four girls in a single-parent household, for me the job became a source of freedom and independence.

Quite naturally the household essentials took precedence over the things most teenagers deemed necessary for adequate socialization. My best friend LaKeiah and I both got hired together and in our eyes, we were about to change our world. It was my first real chance to create a work ethic for myself. I soared and quickly gained the attention of management. I continued working there through high school graduation and was even invited back to work during summers and over holiday breaks once I went away to school.

LaKeiah and I had been best friends since 7th grade so any opportunity to be together was a thrill, even at work. As early trendsetters, we created a system that had our managers looking forward to the magic that we brought to the coveted "drive-through" position on busy weekends. We were a powerful duo even then!

Once going off to college I managed to land several other jobs, including gas station attendant, working in a grocery store deli, and of course a few retail gigs. As an aspiring first-generation college graduate, I felt a great sense of responsibility to finish school, but quite frankly, it was a struggle. My parents, although divorced, did their very best to support me but still more was needed just to survive. Odd jobs were essential to my survival from the start and quickly became part of my norm as a young adult.

In May of 1996 I graduated from my beloved Prairie View A&M University with a Bachelor of Arts Degree in Communications. Graduation was my first real sense of accomplishment in life, and I knew at that moment I had made my entire family proud. Because I had only planned to become a cosmetologist as was my mother, I had never given any major course of study any real thought. Other than my teachers, I did not know one person who was college-educated.

I had entered college as an Undecided major and quickly found an interest in radio/television. Through persistence and patience, the summer prior to graduation I managed to land an internship at one of the most popular stations in the Dallas/Fort Worth metroplex. It was a great experience but led to no real leads for gainful employment after graduation. I always held that hope that it could and knew that my interest in the field would one day work for my good.

At the advice of my father, a dock worker and minister, I was encouraged to pursue a career in teaching as a "back up plan." During that time the education arena was the most recession-proof job one could ever have. He would often say to me, "Radio is fun, but you want to be able to eat." I absolutely agreed. After struggling through undergrad the thought of a steady paycheck bigger than any that I had ever known possible sounded like a master plan.

In the Fall of 1996 I started my teaching career earning a whopping $26,000 a year. I was accepted into what is known as an alternative-certification program in a large urban school district. It was my first professional job and I was terrified and excited at the very same time. I entered the classroom optimistic and confident that I would change the world.

For the next several years I continued to find my way in the classroom. I met some outstanding educators along the way and was able to offer hope through education to countless students. I was young and single and had not lived long enough or extensively enough to have any real comparisons, so things felt normal. By the Fall of 1998 my father had died unexpectedly and I was left totally on my own to find my place in the world and support myself. At the age of 24 I purchased my very first home with the proceeds inherited from his life insurance policy. The vicissitudes of life had introduced me to the real world. I lived a very average life and found that I still was barely making enough to cover my basic living expenses on my teacher's salary. As a result, I kept a side gig to make ends meet. By nature, I have always been a strategist and survivor!

After seven years in the classroom I had grown comfortable. As an inborn leader, I had always managed to gain the attention and favor of those over me. With the blessing of my superiors, I decided to go back to school to pursue a Master's degree in Educational Administration. I believed that once I became an administrator I would have a greater sphere of influence in my school community- and in terms of finances, I would definitely be able to finally let go of all the side jobs I was working to survive.

Getting an advanced degree was indeed the natural progression if I'd ever planned to climb the ladder.

After obtaining a Master's in 2002 I landed my first job as an administrator. At that point I had achieved more in life than anyone else in my immediate and extended family. I was proud of what I had accomplished, but knew there was still much more to come. For the next eight years I worked as an assistant principal under leaders of all types. I learned a great deal about leadership from each one, some extraordinary and some, not so much. I had finally shifted from survival mode to success and for a while, I felt relieved.

By the Fall of 2011 I had matriculated my way through the system to become a campus principal. Never in a million years had I imagined myself as a principal! My goal starting out in 1996 was simply to get a teaching certificate as a "back up plan" based on my father's advice. I had started and never stopped. By this time I was now a married mother of one toddler and expecting my second child. Life was good and I was extremely grateful. I remember in graduate school one of my professors saying, "Your first school is like your first child." I now agreed. Regardless of what others thought, my school was the best thing ever and I was now responsible for its well-being and growth. I thought it was the most beautiful thing ever at the time. In reality my school was among the oldest buildings in the district and needed an overhaul figuratively and literally. After a decade later, I knew firsthand what my professor meant.

As a working mom with a husband who knew all too well the demands of a principal's responsibilities from personal experience, things grew difficult for me to manage. Overseeing the day-to-day operations of a school, which on any given day might include social worker, mental health professional, paramedic, community activist, life coach, priest, peace officer, and even judge, often eclipsed the focus from instructional leadership. Public education had changed and I was not sure if it was going in the right direction for me. My passion to make a difference in education was being redefined. I desired to equip people with the tools to change their lives. I knew that I had been gifted to instruct, impart, and influence, but wasn't so sure that teaching and learning would continue to be in session for me in the confines a school building.

In addition, the constant and sometimes unfounded changes from the district and state levels would leave me at times conflicted. Do we do what's best for students or do we focus on meeting rigorous standards, at any cost? I quickly realized that I was expected to be for my students what I could not be for my own children. My attention had shifted to wanting to be the best parent possible for my own children and to be available for the 'firsts' in our house. Daily I began to ask myself 'is there a way to still earn a living, put family first, and still work in integrity and with passion?'

I remember reading an article that outlined ways to know if your current job was your life's work. One of the indicators that resonated with me stated that your life's work will allow you flexibility and freedom of time to take care of yourself and your family. Getting up at the crack of dawn and winding down close to midnight daily did not really lend itself to a balanced existence! Especially in a situation where I felt that I was no longer challenged and fulfilled. I knew that a life existed whereby I could use my experience, gifts, and talents freely and create an economy for family simultaneously. The idea of becoming a 'passionpreneur' was quite enticing. If the ideal circumstance didn't exist, I was now charged to create it. The search ensued.

During the last two years I worked in schools I felt as if I were living in two different worlds. I was absolutely committed to my career and providing excellent instructional leadership in my building, but I became even more committed to my personal development. I set out to put a name and face to my life's work. Education is noble work, but it was not my life's work- at least not in such a traditional capacity.

I had spent 17 years teaching and leading in schools and was confident that the experience I had gained in the process would forever be a part of me. As I grew more certain that my departure would soon be evident, I worked to prepare my successor for the job without even knowing it. We had always had a great working relationship and friendship too. I absolutely trusted her so I would share the good and the bad about being in the seat. Without even having a detailed exit plan devised, I would always make statements like 'you are going to need to know this when I'm gone' or 'this is something that you may want to change to suit your leadership style when you take my place.' I'm sure she thought I was mentally caving in at times due to the pressure!

However, I have always lived in my future. As I struggled to gain clarity on what mattered most to me in life, I realized that the longer I sat in a space that was no longer a fit for me, the longer I held up the next man's opportunity. I, without reservation, believe that being in a place in life past your appointed time can be just as damaging as being placed there too early. I had to make a move so that I could start my next chapter and the man (in this case woman) waiting on my seat could do the same.

In May of 2012 I summoned the courage to resign my position. It was equally freeing and frightening. I knew precisely what my options would be in terms of advancement if I had continued my course in public school administration. What I did not know yet wanted desperately to learn was the possibilities that existed for me if I opened myself up to something new.

Making the shift was a calculated risk, but a risk nonetheless. I had been offered a chance to work in Public Relations and Marketing for a life insurance company. It was a transition that was easy for me to make because it was home-based and allowed flexibility which was now a top criteria for me as a working mom. It was a great match for my skill set and I was elated to try my hand in a new arena. If I would ever have the courage to jump, the time was now. Financially, it was a cut in pay which was a bit of a concern initially, but I knew that choosing and placing the needs of my family and my own mental well-being at the forefront could never be quantified in terms of a dollar amount. I viewed it as an opportunity to align my priorities. It was bittersweet announcing to my staff that I was moving on, but for the few that knew Mrs. Morrow *the principal* and Stefani *the person*, they applauded my willingness to launch out. Many had privately told me so and longed to do it themselves but lacked the courage to act.

I worked for the insurance company for a little over a year before the opportunity played out. The company decided to close the school market for which I had been hired to help establish due to my expertise in education. On September 30, 2014 I was fired in the most amicable way possible. For the first time ever in my adult life I was now unemployed. It was liberating in a sense to be released from something that no longer served me. I knew going in the job was not designed for the long-term but can recall thinking 15 months was a bit fast! The reality is my house at the time was a double-income household and the initial thought of losing an income was at the onset a bit frightening. While most people would have been devastated, I was actually relieved.

That was the moment I knew had advanced to my next level. I was more afraid of what my life would become if I retreated than I was of answering the call to head in the direction of my future. I had watched the trends in the company during the last six months and knew that the end was nearing before it had actually arrived. I did not want to exert time and energy forcing something that was meant to serve as a bridge into a mainstay. The position was sent to throw me a line to make a move and I had done so. Luckily, I had come to a place in life where I was no longer willing or interested in doing things that were not directly aligned with my destiny. It was a bold stance to take, but turning 40 had made me more apt to take risks. I made a decision at that moment to write this book and to seek a life of total truth that most of the people around me did not know was possible. I knew that my very existence depended on it.

Early on in 2014 I knew the year would be a "light bulb" one for me. I had become confident in the power of my story and the necessity of sharing my experience with the world. It is amazing how the universe moves on your behalf when you become aware of who you are, where you are, what you have, and that which you have been divinely created to do. I was now certain that I been gifted not only to lead, but to inspire and motivate women to be more than they had ever imagined.

Through great conviction, courage, and clarity I had developed a voice of power that people came to know and demand informally and now, formally. I understood that there were people in the earth that were assigned to hear my voice and that I had left them in waiting far too long. It had been a story 40 years in the making and the time to press the "play" button was at hand. Over the past two years I had begun what I coined my 'success studies' where I closely delved into the paths of individuals who had attained massive success in their respective areas of business and in life. In every case, all had launched into the deep waters of destiny not fully understanding HOW their dream would play out, but rather focusing on the fact that it COULD and believing IT WOULD from inception to manifestation. I had become fully convinced that living in personal integrity and sharing my gifts with the world on my terms were both possible and intended to do so the balance of my days.

In this book I will share the life lessons that I relearned as well as new discoveries made in my leap from *principal* to *passionpreneur*, a term that I personally define as, "individuals who use their areas of passion to create viable business models and personal economies." Because of the nature of the 'passion projects' the lives of many individuals are impacted greatly and enriched as a result. These undertakings will require one to access their core and put the needs of those being served at the forefront. Integrity and authenticity are prerequisites. Work of this sort constantly tugs at the heartstrings and its compensation is always an unmatched sense of fulfillment.

I am fueled by my passion. I work daily in a multitude of roles including wife, mother, leader, inspirer, entrepreneur, speaker, coach, and now author. I have spent countless hours engaging in self-development, dialoging with like-minded individuals, self-reflecting, living on purpose, and learning things about myself and the world in which we live. As a business owner, I am my own boss and serve as the CEO of my dream. My work schedule has gone from 7a.m.-5p.m., to whenever I start until whenever it gets done- and I love it!

When making the transition from employee to entrepreneur, I learned one's entire *modus operandi* must change. I do not profess to be an expert of any sort, but rather a woman who has learned some valuable lessons that I now hold as truths. I am certain that mastery of these lessons will help any thinking, open-minded person reduce the time it will take to reach their next level. When I was a teacher I always expected each student to receive a daily "takeaway," and I feel the same way concerning the words written on the proceeding pages. My deepest desire is that these lessons will speak to you, ultimately causing a shift in your thinking and heightened sense of self-awareness.

Changing your life is difficult and can take some time. Know that this book was written to help you **start** the process. Raising your self-perception is undoubtedly the most important step you can take to start the journey. As your mindset begins to shift upwards, all else about you will follow suit. I certainly hope that you will be inspired to make a decision to create your best life **now**. I am headed to the top and will be looking for you to meet me there!

Settle on Success,
Stefani

You will never fulfill your destiny doing work you despise.

-John C. Maxwell

Lesson 1

Clearly identify your dominant talents and gifts.

 Awakening to the realization that a life exists unlike the one you've known can be daunting *and* liberating. Living your best life simply starts by being able to articulate why you are here, what you are to do, and who you are to touch. This notion is clearly outlined by Napoleon Hill as 'definiteness of purpose' in the legendary *Think and Grow Rich*. Hill writes, "Knowing what one wants is the first, and, perhaps most important step toward the development of persistence." Hence, this lesson is strategically placed because being armed with this truth is the only way mentally to position yourself to work meaningfully, realize your dreams and absorb the proceeding lessons. I believe every living person was created with giftings and talents divinely given by God. Some were given more than others, but every person is distributed a measure. What we do with what we have been given determines our future course and the opportunity to experience the multiplicity of our gifts.

If you are self-reflective and growing in consciousness, settling on your dominant area might be a more attainable task. For those that live unaware and unresponsive, discovering your dominance is possibly a bit more elusive. Establishing a 'definiteness of purpose' can be extremely frustrating for individuals that are multi-talented. When you have an inclination to do many things well, honing in on your primary gifts can be challenging. This is what I call the "3T- Effect." You may make great tacos, fix flat tires and prepare taxes all at the same time and in the same business. However, everything you have a knack for doing is not a part of your ultimate purpose in life. Some gifts are to be merely enjoyed or work in alignment with other more dominant ones. Identifying and focusing on one area will help you to minimize distractions and avoid overworking yourself.

I have always had an eye for interior design. Creating a welcoming environment in my home has always been a priority. In times past people who have come to our home have asked for my help to design their personal space. After multiple requests to create spaces and failed attempts to start a design business, I finally realized it was not my dominant gift. While I enjoy it and do it well enough to be handsomely compensated, it is simply not the thing that I wake up with in the morning or carry to bed with me each night.

Of course trying your hand in various areas until you find what works for you is absolutely natural. You owe it to yourself to try; just be sure to remain perceptive and forward thinking. Often through those failed attempts you find your way to your true area of passion. I term this "failing forward," and it is a part of the process I will discuss in a subsequent lesson.

By the way, don't be discouraged or moved by those who live to snatch the dreams of others. Expect that there will be some who mock your varied attempts to find what fits you. The reality is if these people had the courage and capacity to seek their own dreams, they would not have time to criticize yours. It was through a 40- year exploration that I found my answers. I was able to gain clarity after realizing the things I *did not* want for my life just as much as what I actually *desired*. I am able now to understand and articulate that my passion and purpose is to expose, equip, and empower others (especially women) to create a more fulfilled existence. Writing this book is only one of the many ways in which I'll share my gift with the world.

Let us not forget about those well-meaning friends and relatives that create labels and categories based on how *they* perceive your gifts and talents, further clouding the process. Making a determination solely based on what others think, say, or believe is highly unadvised. I cannot list the people that I know personally that have found themselves trapped in situations because they attempt to uphold a vision designed by others for their life. If you are not committed to living in integrity and using your own voice, you can find yourself working in areas in which you are *talented*, but not *passionate*. I have learned to vote for passion- it keeps you motivated in tough times.

I advise you not to waste time and energy attempting to monetize everything that you have ever done well. Instead, look within for your dominant gift or ability. From the vantage point of a person that has multiple gifts, I can tell you that you'll know the "dominant one" when you feel it. It is the one area, when utilized in conjunction with secondary ones will produce magic. It is the area to which all of your other gifts and talents can be linked. It is the birthplace of your passion. It is the thing that you do naturally, most times with little or no training or coaching.

You might even be able to go back into your childhood to find traces of its inception. It is the thing that you envision yourself doing that may be so far from your present reality, that you are afraid to even share with those around you, fearing ridicule. It is what resonates with you and is fueled by a creative energy that cannot be explained at times or quantified monetarily. Do not be confused by what you are *paid to do* via your career or job, but rather gain absolute clarity about you were *made to do*. Know that your gift was created to be shared with the world. It will serve others in ways unimaginable. It is paramount that you identify exactly what *it is* and precisely what it *is not*. You will live in frustration and defeat until you do so.

I will end this lesson and all subsequent ones with a list of questions designed to start a mental shift and to challenge your thinking as you embark upon your path to your next level. Use the space provided to answer each question as truthfully and thoroughly as possible. Use the self-reflection space to capture additional thoughts or realizations you may have after internalizing each lesson.

Guiding Questions:

- What product or service do you create with so much enjoyment that you would do it free of charge, but you do it so masterfully others have offered to pay you for it?

- What skill set comes to you naturally and effortlessly? What are your areas of struggle?

- What would you do with your time each day if money or the lack thereof was a non-issue?

"Hide not your talents. They for use were made. What's a sundial in the shade?" -**Benjamin Franklin**

Lesson 1 Self- Reflection Notes

_____

_____

_____

_____

_____

_____

_____

_____

_____

_____

_____

_____

_____

_____

_____

_____

_____

_____

_____

_____

_____

_____

_____

_____

_____

_____

_____

_____

_____

_____

_____

_____

_____

_____

_____

_____

_____

_____

_____

_____

_____

_____

_____

_____

_____

_____

Lesson 2

Expect to hear *no* and experience some failure.

WHENEVER YOU decide to do something extraordinary with your life know that hearing "No" along the way is part of the process. Anticipate it. Most of the people around you will never launch out and try their hand at anything other than what they are comfortable doing because they fear failure, being judged, and being told **no**. I am constantly amazed at how people can more steadfastly hold true to the opinions of others over their own convictions. The small-minded thinking of "playing it safe" is especially alluring because no risk is involved. Limited thinking is the birthplace of low-risk living, not to mention the uncomfortable reality of *perceived* comfort zones. Besides, do you really want to forego the opportunity to achieve greatness based on the opinions of someone whose reality is simply maintaining the status quo?

I believe real power exists in understanding this lesson because doing so can take away the stigma of failure. If you *know* that failure is likely to occur at some point along the way, you are not as prone to unravel completely when it does occur. You are able to better manage your way past barriers, evaluate errors in your process and hit the reset button as needed, always focused on your end result. Any person that has created a life worth mentioning had to navigate their way through countless closed doors and failed attempts, all while maintaining the hope that their derailed dream would someday be realized.

And don't be frightened to know that you may even lose some money during the process. You have got to be okay with taking some calculated financial risks. You can't expect others to believe in a dream that you are not convicted enough to invest in yourself. I'm not suggesting that you get a five-figure loan every time you have an idea. I am saying that you must be willing to invest in your dreams and not crucify yourself if you lose money in the process. As you begin to familiarize yourself with the paths of those having achieved massive success in any field, you won't help but notice the trends.

When I decided to transition from being a principal and went to work for the insurance company I can remember countless people asking, "So what will you do if it doesn't work out for you?" I would always respond by saying 'What if it does and I miss an opportunity to change my life because I did not try?' Although I was uncertain of the path ahead, I believed changing the trajectory of my life held just as much promise of success as it did failure. After all, I had always believed that I *really was* born to win, even when I didn't know *how* to win.

In times past I thought hearing the word **no** meant I was pursuing an endeavor that was simply not for me. I had always relented when I encountered less than favorable feedback. During my upbringing I had been conditioned to believe the doors of opportunity opened easily and to retreat at the first sign of resistance, not making any waves in life. This behavior and mindset is based on false teaching that suggests that "what's mine or meant for me will freely and without friction will come to me" when actually the polar opposite is indeed true. You must whole-heartedly and very passionately pursue arriving at your elevated place in life and doing so is hard! What I had failed to learn is that the doors of opportunity worth entering are usually closed, yet those who are persistent and courageous knock at them without ceasing until they are open. Sometimes **no** really means **not now**. You must be attuned to your inner-self to know the difference. I've come to understand that the rejection you encounter en route to your best life is really designed to test your resilience and ultimately determine your willingness to pay the price to reach the top.

There is one caveat to this lesson that I must share. There are times that **no** simply means **no**, not today, not ever. Do not ignore attempts to do things that are futile and not divinely assigned for your life. Do not waste your time and energy trying to force things to happen that are not authentic to who you are at your core and therefore do not resonate with you. Though opposition is a part of the process, making progress should not be impossible.

This is the concept of forcing a square peg in a round hole. The universe knows your capacity to receive and will not deliver that which is not yours. If you are on the right track you will be fueled by your passion and doors will begin to open for you. This is why clarity of purpose and a heightened sense of self are imperative. This is a determination only you can make from true self-reflection. While feedback from those with your best interest in mind helps, knowing where to exert your time and talent is ultimately on you. Don't spin your wheels doing something that you are not passionate about. After all, you are pursuing *your* dream.

Guiding Questions:

- Are you absolutely certain you are pursuing the area of passion that is authentic to who you are? Why or why not? If so, identify and explain.

- When you face resistance while attempting to explore and work outside your comfort zone, what is your first response when you encounter obstacles? Do you proceed or quit trying?

- Do you understand the concept of failing forward? Explain the concept in your own words. In what area of your life are you failing forward?

"If you're not failing every now and again, it's a sure sign you're not doing anything very innovative."
~ Woody Allen

Lesson 2 Self-Reflection Notes

_____

_____

_____

_____

_____

_____

_____

_____

_____

_____

_____

_____

_____

_____

_____

_____

_____

_____

_____

_____

Lesson 3

Ride with opportunity - you never know where it may take you.

 THIS LESSON is particularly special to me because I met the love of my life as a result of taking advantage of an opportunity that I was afforded. During my time in education I was working in a school district where I had been promoted and gained a reputation as an outstanding educator. I was in a position on a campus where I had great support and things were going well, or so I thought. Literally, without provocation this ideal experience came to a screeching halt. I was suddenly being scrutinized and antagonized, thus creating a very hostile working environment.

I have always been able to get along in tough times but given the nature of the accusations I wasn't so sure about this situation. The level of discomfort became so unbearable that I actively began seeking employment elsewhere. It was like I had suddenly outgrown a pair of shoes that were once very comfortable. I knew that remaining in such an environment would be professional and intellectual suicide. I was not willing to take that risk and I realized I did have options, so I began to plot my transition.

I was young, smart, adaptable, and very good at my job and I knew it. I had started the application process for several nearby school districts but only managed to get one completed. It was for a district I had heard of in a nearby town that I knew very little about. Within days of submitting the application I got a call for an interview. My plan had already started to work. I was certain if I got a chance to interview I could captivate the panel and the position would be mine. I was so sure this was the life-changing opportunity I longed for, I went to work the next day and began clearing out my office that evening once everyone left the building. I even typed my resignation letter and left the date blank. When I got the green light I wanted to be ready to part ways immediately!

I never shall forget the Tuesday morning of the interview. When I went in to interview the boxes that I'd packed from my office the day prior were still in the trunk of my car. As I had supposed, the interview panel was impressed with me and I became one of two finalists. I was called in for a second interview Wednesday morning with the superintendent who was asked to help make the selection, and received a call Thursday evening offering me the position. I filled the date in on the resignation letter I had written in faith and gladly delivered it to Human Resources bright and early Friday morning.

That moment was paramount for me because for the first time ever, I had made a decision not be walked over and mistreated in the workplace. I needed to work to support myself, but I could live without all the drama that had become a part of my daily routine. I drove away feeling relieved and looking towards my future and drove directly into it. To my surprise, the person that actually called and offered me the job that fateful Thursday evening became my husband a few years later! Today we share a wonderful marriage and have created a family that we cherish. I had no idea going in that making that one decision would be such a major piece of my life's puzzle.

Opportunity usually has an unfamiliar look on the surface. So many times an opportunity is passed over because we don't recognize the package or because we are unable to see the contents of the package aligning itself with the big picture we have for our life- so we miss it. This is why opening yourself to receive new experiences is so important. Do not make the mistake of being overly consumed with a million "what if" questions, and playing out all the worst-case scenarios in your mind. Instead, develop a 'what if it **does** work' mentality. Dare to see the big picture and analyze whether or not an opportunity has the capacity to move you closer to your dream in some way.

How many times have you squandered a chance to do something great or even different simply because your mind was closed? A missed opportunity can significantly impede your progress, mainly because of the narrow-minded thinking that causes you to be unresponsive. Limited thinking is the real thief that robs us of taking risks and living our best life. What if I had passed on going to work in that district because I didn't know anyone there or did not know much about the town? I made the decision to move based on the big picture that I had for my life at that time. I knew that where I was no longer a fit for me and change was desperately needed. I was not sure that things would work out as they did but **I was willing to take a risk.** I figured remaining in that familiar and emotionally taxing situation was an even greater **risk**.

By no means am I suggesting that you allow yourself to be carried away by every wind and wave presented. I am suggesting that you begin to take risks and do some things you've not tried before. You must be able to determine which opportunities deserve a real look and are worth your time and energy. An adult is presumed to possess a certain measure of common sense and maturity, so use it to empower and enable you to properly recognize and leverage opportunities.

If you are ever to get to a new place in life you must begin to explore new opportunities. In order to do so you must work to raise your level of thinking in order to be able to hear and see more clearly as opportunities are made available to you. This is a process that starts by first realizing and acknowledging that your current views are somewhat limited.

Next, commit to remove those limitations. Learn to take chances and know that risk and reward are always congruent. Be gentle and give yourself the time and space to grow into being a more open-minded and perceptive individual. All too often we are our own saboteurs because we refuse to embrace change. Rather than revert to negativity by default the next time you are presented with a new opportunity, refuse to make a decision based on what you *think* you know. Try to remain open and actually *consider* the possibilities. You never know if the opportunity will ultimately become an integral piece of your life's puzzle. Stay open and stay conscious!

Guiding Questions:

- Have there been opportunities to create a better life that you *know* you've missed? If so, list them and identify the level of consciousness in which you existed at that time, causing you to do so.

- On a scale of 1 to 10 (with 10 being the highest) rate your willingness to embrace change. What practical, deliberate steps can you take to raise your rating?

- What do you fear most about new situations? Why? What practical, deliberate steps can you take to mitigate your fear?

"If someone offers you an amazing opportunity and you're not sure you can do it, say yes- then learn how to do it later."-**Richard Branson**

Lesson 3 Self-Reflection Notes

Lesson 4

An overdue delivery carries just as many risks as a premature birth.

I LIKEN this lesson to women and the miracle of childbirth. As a mother, I understand the joy of carrying a child. I was blessed to give birth to two bundles of joy; for the first time at age 35 and again at 38. I became a mother somewhat later than I previously anticipated for my life, but divine providence trumped my plans.

Though motherhood is a rewarding experience it can be emotionally taxing to await the delivery of an unborn child. I have never been a fan of pain so I agonized as I played out different scenarios in my head concerning the actual delivery. Every single day I was ever so careful to do my best to follow the doctor's orders by eating properly, getting ample rest and avoiding stressful situations as much as possible.

When you are expecting a baby you live in a constant state of uncertainty mixed with excitement. You hear heart-breaking stories about babies being born prematurely, struggling to survive because they were not fully developed. These stories can be unnerving, even for a person of great faith. My own mother's first-born daughter was born six weeks prematurely and later passed away from complications. On the other side of that coin is the instance where a baby can be left in the womb too long, thus complicating the delivery and putting the mother and child both in grave danger. Sometimes overdue deliveries can result in brain damage, and in some cases even death. Even when an expectant mother has done everything by the book the experience can end in less than favorable conditions.

I believe giving birth to a dream it is much like giving birth to a child. For an extended period of time you carry your baby and all the hope of its future everywhere you go until it makes its entrance on the earth. Your dream must be protected with the same care and diligence you would devote to your unborn child. The closer it gets to the due date, the more uncomfortable life becomes. You feel as though you are about to explode with creative gushes and can no longer contain your gift to yourself.

You and you alone bear the task of delivering that dream in the earth. Others will help you along the way, but ultimately it must come through you. Your family and friends may be cheering you along in the waiting room, but they are not allowed in the delivery room. Know that there may only be a select, privileged few to watch you *give birth* because **the birthing room is no place for spectators.**

The ideas and dreams that come to you can only come through you. You and only you were appointed to give it life. The same travailing that takes place in childbirth is present when you give birth to your dream. Once your dream is realized it has to be nursed daily and can require around the clock care. There is a new level of accountability and responsibility that you must embrace if you intend for your dream to ever fully function. You must watch over it and commit yourself to its growth just as you would your infant child. What your dream becomes depends on what you put into its upbringing.

As with the child that is born too early, your dream can be short-lived if it is exposed to the world before time. If your dream has not been built up and fortified, it cannot stand. There is a gestation period that you must allow to happen naturally from the moment you gain absolute clarity and the time you actually present your gift to the world. That clarity is evident when you can articulate specifically what your dream entails. You should know what it is you desire to do and be able to identify the lives you intend to touch in doing so. A certain level of growth and maturity is needed to get you off to a solid start. Setting out ill-prepared can cost you everything. Don't get in a hurry and press "play" too soon. You know you are moving too soon if you:

- Cannot clearly articulate your vision or that vision is constantly changing

- Are too afraid to take risks

- Don't have a follow-up plan

I know that wanting to go ahead and get started is tempting when you believe supply and demand has been created, thus causing you to want to launch out immediately. Take the time to determine the particulars of how your gift can be best expressed, always focusing on the details. The minor details can be the difference in someone of influence saying *yes* or *no* to your work.

Work diligently to create the most authentic and meaningful expression of your dream. Doing so can set you apart from all the rest.

I believe that if you are self-aware, you will know when it is time- don't wait for others to tell you. Self-awareness is cultivated through constant reflection, assessment, and introspection. Get to know yourself in a way that you've not known prior. Spend some time exploring and growing. Learn what makes you unique and develop a new level of self-confidence in your abilities. Because I had began to operate at a certain level of awareness I was able to perceive the timing window for myself in my own life. For the first time I was clear on what it was I aspired to do and the impact I knew such work would make in the world. I knew that the time to move had arrived. There's a confidence that is created in your stillness that will alert you.

One sure indication that the time is near is when housing the gift inside you becomes unbearable. Your levels of creativity and avenues for expression will be at an all-time high. It is as though the load you are carrying is too much to handle and letting it out is the only way to find relief. Be extremely cautious and do not mistake this feeling with impatience and move before time with a half-done plan of half-hearted effort. When the time comes there will be an indescribable push to just get it out. There's a level of energy and confidence that will appear, thus giving you strength to push. Remember, timing will never be absolutely perfect. Instead of waiting for all the pieces to perfectly align, listen to yourself for inner cues.

I do believe firmly in divine timing, but I also know that procrastination, fear, self-doubt, limiting beliefs, lack of clarity and creativity, and being overly concerned about what others think of you can put you behind in realizing your dreams. Regardless of your season of life, it is never too late to pursue your dream, yet think of it this way- would you rather enjoy the fruits of success and live a life of abundance and significance for 5 years or 25 years? Don't spend countless years roaming and wandering, wishing and hoping. Find the courage to actively pursue your dream and prepare for delivery sooner than later. Your water is about to break. Remember, someone is waiting on you to introduce your dream to the world!

Guiding Questions:

- What are some possible solutions available to you to help remove barriers in being able to determine *when* to move on your dream?

- How has limited-thinking kept you from making progress in determining *when* you will move or act?

- Are you behind on presenting your gift to the world? If not, where are you in your timetable? If so, clearly outline the reasons why. What active steps can you take to get on track?

"Make your move before you are ready. Leap and grow your wings on the way down." - **Les Brown**

Lesson 4 Self-Reflection Notes

_____

_____

_____

_____

_____

_____

_____

_____

_____

_____

_____

_____

_____

_____

_____

_____

_____

_____

_____

_____

Stefani McDade Morrow

_____
_____
_____
_____
_____
_____
_____
_____
_____
_____
_____
_____
_____
_____
_____
_____
_____
_____
_____
_____
_____
_____
_____
_____
_____

Lesson 5

Nominate yourself for greatness-it's your responsibility.

 YOU SINGLE-HANDEDLY possess the power to create a bigger, better life for yourself. So many times we give that responsibility to a spouse, our children, certain friends, and even our careers. Fulfilling your destiny is too great an undertaking to delegate. I believe that most people really think there is *someone* or *something* else keeping them from moving forward. Just ask a few of your friends what's keeping them from really leaving their mark in the world. Many will respond by faulting entities outside of themselves. The reality is your self-imposed limitations are more powerful than all outside factors combined.

I too was guilty of assigning blame to the *secondary* conditions in my life as the rationale for me being stuck, not fully realizing that the gifts and talents given to me at birth were unchanging and therefore primary. I had everything backwards. Our *circumstances* in life are conditional and can change at any given moment, therefore making them a poor lens through which to see ourselves and particularly our future. Only until I realized that regardless of the conditions around me, I still had what it took on the inside (my innate talents and abilities) to move my life forward. With that realization, *I nominated myself* for greatness. I accepted complete responsibility for my happiness and fulfillment.

Sadly, lifetimes have come and gone while some have waited for *others* to make life-changing choices for them. The decision to experience life's best is very personal and can only be made by you and for you. If you don't vote for you, do really think that others will be inclined to do so? If you are waiting by the phone for someone to call and validate who you are and what you have been given, and **give you permission** to succeed in life, just know that you might be waiting for a long while.

When you share your gifts with the world, developing a sense of entitlement may seem contradictory. Too often entitlement is associated with being greedy, self-serving, and even wicked. I view entitlement as deserving of the opportunity to share your gifts and talents with the world. This is the one time in life being selfish is not only allowed but required. You were given your gifts and talents to be used, not to be hidden from the world in fear and doubt. Here's a newsflash- in order to be at the top, you've got to see yourself at the top and believe *you have a right* to be there. Do know however getting to the top will require you to cooperate and collaborate with people who will make their way into your life when you start moving. You will absolutely have to depend on others to *help* execute your vision, but the outcome is yours.

Remember, you do not serve the world or yourself by downplaying who you are and what you have to offer. False humility will only keep you underachieving. The very fact you are willing to pay the price to get to the top *qualifies* you to be there, because most people simply won't pay the price. They choose to hold on to their self-imposed alibis rather than create a new reality. You have to recognize the worth that you bring to a situation and walk in assurance. Don't be swayed by the small minds that mistake confidence for arrogance. You have to believe living a fulfilled life is not only *attainable*, but *allowable*. No sin or law exists against not only sharing your gifts and talents to help others, but making a profit in the process. If you make the decision to create a better life and put in the leg-work to see it through, you deserve to enjoy the fruits of your labor. If living your dream is not for you, then who else might you suggest? Experiencing the fullness that comes along with making your dream a reality is definitely for me and for you too if you so desire.

Guiding Questions:

- Have you ever been guilty of blaming others or your circumstances as the reason you are not moving forward?

- What are the areas in your life in which you need to redirect your focus from blaming others to assuming **personal responsibility**?

- Do you feel worthy of living a life that others have only dreamed of? What is one active step you can take today toward attaining that life?

"Concern yourself more with accepting responsibility than with assigning blame. Let the possibilities inspire you more than the obstacles discourage you."
-Ralph Marston

Lesson 5 Self-Reflection Notes

_____

_____

_____

_____

_____

_____

_____

_____

_____

_____

_____

_____

_____

_____

_____

_____

_____

_____

_____

Stefani McDade Morrow

_____

_____

_____

_____

_____

_____

_____

_____

_____

_____

_____

_____

_____

_____

_____

_____

_____

_____

_____

_____

_____

_____

_____

_____

_____

_____

Lesson 6

Everything that is available is not accessible.

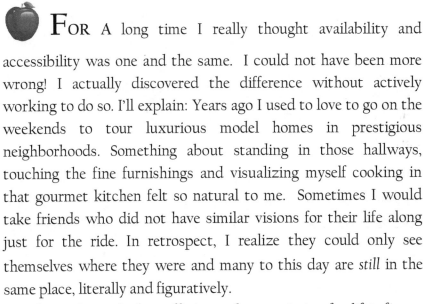 FOR A long time I really thought availability and accessibility was one and the same. I could not have been more wrong! I actually discovered the difference without actively working to do so. I'll explain: Years ago I used to love to go on the weekends to tour luxurious model homes in prestigious neighborhoods. Something about standing in those hallways, touching the fine furnishings and visualizing myself cooking in that gourmet kitchen felt so natural to me. Sometimes I would take friends who did not have similar visions for their life along just for the ride. In retrospect, I realize they could only see themselves where they were and many to this day are *still* in the same place, literally and figuratively.

I have always had an affinity and appreciation for life's finest, regardless of my zip code. Dream building is still a relaxing pastime for me and offers me exposure to the next levels. However, most of the sought after neighborhoods were always nestled away in remote areas and many of them were in gated communities. In order to get into the secured community I needed to know the code to get on the other side of the gate. It didn't matter how well I was dressed or what I was driving- *no code, no entry.* As I was finding my way on my new path to actualizing my dreams, I thought back to these experiences and the reality of the importance of the "code" became instantly clear. Perusing the outskirts of the neighborhood was available to anyone that drove by. **Getting through the gate and ultimately into the model home (which was my goal) required having the code.** Everyone on the other side of that gate knew something that I did not, and what *they* knew was the code. I could not be granted access unless I was able to provide the code.

One of the first steps for me in deciding to pursue my dream and to achieve success at high levels in all areas of my life was realizing that it was actually possible. Even though most of those around me had been satisfied conforming to the status quo, there was always a deep desire within me to do and become more. Know that having a bigger vision for your life automatically puts distance between you and those that do not have the courage to do the same.

I had always been blessed to have really great, hard-working people in my life. When I examined what they all had accomplished there were countless similarities in their stories. They all had great jobs, nice homes, and functional families for the most part. They had achieved what most might call the "good life." While I too coveted the "good life" in times past, I later realized there was a "great life" waiting to be discovered and only lived by a daring few. To strike out on that sparsely populated path required a great deal of courage.

I wanted to live a life filled with passion but did not know *how*. I desperately wanted to get on the other side of that gate, which for me represented my purpose-filled life. I simply did not have the code. I had been denied access to my best life just as I had been denied access at the gate trying to get in to walk through those mansions. It was *available* to me because I desired it, but it was not *accessible* to me because I did not know what to do to obtain it.

Learning the code is where the breakdown occurs for most. They have the desire but never put themselves in a position to learn what it takes to gain access. The code is simply learning and mastering the principles and systems of success. There are no secrets. Those living a life of true significance have at some point learned and applied these principles, thus being granted their own version of the code. You learn the code by consciously making choices and taking advantage of new opportunities. While the path for every person is unique, I now realize the element of choice is always a recurring theme on the road to your best life. Living a life of passion is available to anyone who is willing to learn the code- and thus the code is open to us all. Do away with the thought that there are only a select few people in life who are allowed to have access. **You** can be in that number if you choose to.

At times the situations and circumstances of life may indicate that some possess an unfair advantage in gaining access in comparison to others, but remember, **choice is always the great equalizer.** On my journey I discovered that every living person, whether acknowledged or not, has been given the gift of free will. It is part of our divinely created DNA. That gift has the capacity to produce both good and bad, and is always at the mercy of its carrier. Regardless of where a person starts, living their dream is possible and the choice is theirs.

Think about the countless rags to riches stories you've heard down through the years. Some people have been born into meager, impoverished situations and make their way out to create incredible lives, leaving the world in awe. How does this happen? Everything begins with a choice. Successful people were granted access to their next level through the choices they made. They made a decision, took the time to learn the systems and principles governing success and put them to work in their lives. We have also heard of those who were born with the proverbial "silver spoon," and in spite of their privileged upbringing end up on skid row as a result of a string of bad choices. The media manages daily to provide us with countless examples of them - just turn on the television. These people were off to a great start in life but lost their way ultimately because of poor choices.

So you see where or how you start doesn't matter. What matters is knowing that living your dream is not only **possible** but also *available* to you today. You must make the decision and be willing to put in the work to make your dream *accessible* to you. Achieving accessibility is what separates the haves from the have-nots!

Guiding Questions:

- What are some areas in life that you believe you have been restricted from accessing? Examine those areas. In what ways are those areas directly influenced by choices you made in the past or are presently making?

- What are some activities in which you can engage **today** to help gain access to your dream?

- Do you really believe choice is ultimately the deciding factor for those who achieve in comparison to those who do not? Explain why or why not.

"Today knowledge has power. It controls access to opportunity and advancement." -**Peter Drucker**

Lesson 6 Self-Reflection Notes

_____

_____

_____

_____

_____

_____

_____

_____

_____

_____

_____

_____

_____

_____

_____

_____

_____

_____

_____

_____

_____

_____

_____

_____

_____

_____

_____

_____

_____

_____

_____

_____

_____

_____

_____

_____

_____

_____

_____

_____

_____

_____

_____

Lesson 7

Give people ownership of their opinion of you.

 ONE OF my most valuable lessons learned to date was figuring out that what other people think about me *really is* none of my business. You experience a feeling of freedom once you really gain the courage to release yourself from others' imprisoning ideas about how your life should be. What I found is that most people profess freedom with their words but still remain bound in their behavior. Finding yourself influenced by what those close to you think about you or the choices you make is very common. There is a divide that begins to appear when the thoughts of others no longer coincide with the thoughts that you have about yourself, especially as you begin to grow and expand your self-perception. You might find yourself at an impasse. You can either choose to chart a new course for yourself regardless of what others think, which is what I personally recommend. The other choice is to remain a slave to the low expectations that others have created for you, often times in alignment with their own.

What I find really strange is our willingness to give our power to people who have not created for themselves lives we can to look to for inspiration. Many times people are afraid to take risks or endeavor to do new things because of how they think they will be perceived by others. How often have you secretly asked yourself, 'I wonder what my mom, dad, husband, sister, etc. would think about me trying this?' You fail to stop and realize that someone's opinion of an area in which they have no experience cannot be justly qualified, and should never be a determining factor *for you*. You would not seek parenting advice from a childless individual or investing tips from a person with no access to money. So why would you allow people who are not living their dream to weigh in on you living yours?

I too was guilty of this destructive pattern until I adopted a new thought process. When I decided to pursue my life's passion I realized that I personally only knew of a few people that had actually done so. I soon understood that only the people that had done with their life what I desired to do in my own possessed the right to have an opinion about me- at least one that I cared to consider. It was a liberating experience for me and it happened over time as I began to take inventory of my relationships. I had been expecting the people in my circle to encourage me in pursuing my dreams while many of them had not done so themselves. I relieved them of that responsibility by putting my own opinions and the opinions of people whose work in life I valued at the top of the list.

You must realize that your opinion of yourself is more important, powerful, and compelling than all other opinions combined. Too often we value what others believe about us and doubt our own individual beliefs. We trust *their words* but not *our own thoughts*. **We dance to their beat but ignore our own music.**

Looking for external validation is extremely dangerous. It sets the stage for blame, placing the responsibility for our personal outcomes with someone else which is always counterproductive. Make every effort to remain in the driver's seat of your life, believing and knowing that *your* voice matters most. Silencing naysayers and critics can be a real chore at times. At first you will consciously have to silence them until you learn to trust yourself and understand your worth. Eventually, this process will begin to happen more naturally.

Allowing others to cast doubt in our hearts and sabotage our chances of living our dream is something we can overcome. I know firsthand because I have done it in my own life. No, I'm not oblivious to the negative chatter about me. Rather, I now know that the only power negativity really has in my life is the power I assign to it. So I make a choice every single day to give full attention to *my* voice and the voices of those who build me, and absolutely no attention to the voices seeking to tear me down.

Guiding Questions:

- Have you ever been guilty of letting the opinions of others inhibit you or prevent you from becoming more? Identify and list the people and their limiting opinions.

- Why do you value others' words about your life over your own?

- What are practical steps you can take to increase your sense of self-worth and value your voice?

"I have often wondered how it is that every man loves himself more than all the rest of men, but yet sets less value on his own opinions of himself than on the opinions of others." - **Marcus Aurelius**

Lesson 7 Self-Reflection Notes

_____

_____

_____

_____

_____

_____

_____

_____

_____

_____

_____

_____

_____

_____

_____

_____

_____

_____

_____

_____

_____

_____

_____

_____

_____

_____

_____

_____

_____

_____

_____

_____

_____

_____

_____

_____

_____

_____

_____

_____

_____

_____

_____

_____

Lesson 8

You already have what it takes ...look inside for it.

I LIKE to think of this lesson in terms of an earthly parent. On my new journey my work now requires me to travel quite a bit. Every time that I am scheduled to be away I make sure I prepare my family for my absence, especially my children. As their mother I believe I know their needs better than any other person alive, at times even more than their father does. Let me say my husband is extremely nurturing and takes exceptional care of our children. Nevertheless as mothers, because of our God-given instinctive and protective nature when it comes to our young, I believe that we sometimes do a more in-depth job of caring for them, regardless of how well others assist us.

I have a wonderful support system yet I always carry the load, at least emotionally, when it comes to my children's well-being. I know I must make sure that the kitchen is well-stocked with not only the staples, but all of the snack and treats they enjoy- and that list can be extensive. With great care I prepare and set out their school clothes, often even down to their socks. I make provisions for their socialization if I will be away for more than day or two by arranging play dates with close friends and trusted caretakers. Clean linens on the bed, books for story time and comfy pajamas make the list too. I mentally play through tons of scenarios over and over again to ensure all their needs will be met while I am away. I always leave everything *in* the house so they'll never have to go or look outside.

And so it is in life, at least for some. My personal belief is we're all created by God, and as a Heavenly Father He has done a most supreme job of leaving *in* us all that we would ever need to live our best life. In His infinite wisdom, He knew to create us in such a way that we would embody and personally house our own treasures. Thankfully, our gifts are placed internally and were never meant to be at the mercy of external forces. Regardless of the details I leave for caregivers, at times I still receive calls because something has been moved around, lost, or simply misplaced. By the same token, if what we need to win has been placed within, why are so many looking around outside trying to find it?

So many times we are guilty of looking externally to validate inner longings because we don't even know what we possess. I too lost irretrievable time on my journey as I looked for answers in the wrong places. Until my self-perception shifted I did not realize the tools I needed to excel were already nestled away, deep down on the inside. I was looking *around* when I should have been looking *within.*

Although God brought people into my life to help in the process with implementation, I possessed my own blueprint. Before they could assist in any way, I had to be clear about what I had, what I desired to accomplish and specifically the type of support needed. Those clarifications came through self-study and introspection. The challenge for many is that with the passing of time life happens and the blueprint becomes increasingly more difficult to locate. The noisy and fast-paced tendency of life can keep you highly frustrated and feeling as though you are moving through your days like an octopus on roller-skates.

You become so bogged down with your daily routine that you really don't know who you are or what you have, let alone how to share your passion with the world. By the time you give pieces of yourself away to your spouse, your children, your employer, your friends and whoever else needs a part of you, it is very easy to have nothing left. This is why living your best life is so crucial. There is a level of mental health I believe personally derives from knowing what you have to share with the world and finding how it fits for you. You can attain the *peace* that comes with knowing your *piece*. You have been granted exclusive access to all the pieces that comprise your life's work. You will never be able to share that work unless you assemble the pieces.

Today I encourage you to find your center and begin to quieten your life so that you can locate what you need to begin your work. You will have to make a very deliberate effort to steal away in the midst of your daily noise. We all have the same 24 hours in a day so you will need to make a real attempt to make each moment count.

Guiding Questions:

- Have you ever been guilty of looking outside of yourself for answers or validation regarding your gifts and talents? If so, explain why.

- Do you fully believe you innately possess all you need to move your life to the next level? Explain why or why not.

- What are some of the reasons you believe looking to external sources for answers is easier than looking within?

"God didn't have time to make a nobody, only a somebody. I believe that each of us has God-given talents within us waiting to be brought to fruition."
-Mary Kay Ash

Lesson 8 Self-Reflection Notes

_____

_____

_____

_____

_____

_____

_____

_____

_____

_____

_____

_____

_____

_____

_____

_____

_____

_____

_____

Lesson 9

A weak WHY won't win.

WHENEVER YOU make the decision to follow your dreams you must have a strong WHY serving as your utmost motivation. This is a part of the growth process that is often overlooked and underestimated in terms of its lasting impact. If you develop a bullet proof reason, you will be fortified enough to withstand the opposition. Your reasons for making the tough choices necessary to your change your life must be bigger than yourself, with service to mankind (in some way) always the focal point. In fact, your WHY should be so compelling and so huge that the thought of making your dreams a reality frightens you. Not to the point of paralysis, but rather being so huge in scope you *know* you will have to depend on a source higher than yourself to pull it off. Your WHY will serve as your daily motivation when you are challenged along the way- remember, you will be. Your WHY has to be a reason that will keep you focused and grounded whenever you consider retreating, either literally or mentally.

A real *why* must be intrinsically driven and pure in motive. For some, it could be to provide a better future for their family. Others may seek to create a life of freedom that makes the idea of having options in life a real possibility. Better schools, better health care and better living conditions for the underserved might be at the core for some. One thing is sure, when your *why* is solid, the *how* does not matter. Hopefully by now you know to anticipate some bumps in the road, detours and delays, and even having to make a few U-turns as you navigate the process of building your dream. Regardless of the direction in which your process takes you and the amount of time it takes to arrive, you must be consistent in holding on to your *why*. It is the compass that will always lead as long as you are willing to follow.

For me, using my voice to help light the path for others is my principal *why*. My *why* forms the sole inspiration for writing this book and seeking to share my story with the world. I know in my soul there are countless individuals in my path who feel trapped and unfulfilled in life and have no idea how to attain a sense of freedom. After going through the process and redefining myself, I feel a great sense of obligation to share with others the truths that have forever changed my course. Doing so can and will help to improve the quality of life for others. I know there are people who need my message because I talk to them almost every single day. Old friends, relatives and even former colleagues ask me about my journey all the time. *How did you get out? What made you do something different? Weren't you afraid to do something you'd never done before? Do you have regrets or miss where you were?* Those are just a few of the most frequently made inquiries about my new life as a passionpreneur. Though some are simply prying, others genuinely want to know if there really is more to life and if so, how to get it.

As you work to develop your own genuine *why*, let me caution you to remove money from the equation. Though securing a financial future can be a byproduct of engaging in such work, this should not be the sole motivation. You will find that if anything other than loving or serving others is at the core, your way of engaging in the process will be tainted and short-lived. When people are driven solely by money, the moment they don't benefit, their level of interest and commitment dissipates. In my opinion, this motivating factor is what differentiates the employee-mind from the entrepreneur-mind. I can certainly admit that as a former employee I expected to receive a paycheck for an agreed upon amount on a designated date, period. Anything else would have definitely presented a problem for all parties involved!

During those days I was working on someone else's dream and that comes with a different set of rules. When your own personal work of passion or dream is on the line, at the beginning you work sometimes without getting paid right away. Perfecting your gifts and talents will take time. If you are passionate, creative and innovative you stand a much better chance of using your passion to create for yourself a viable business model. This will ultimately be determined through supply and demand. In *Think and Grow Rich* author Napoleon Hill writes, "One of the strange things about human beings is that they value only that which has a price." Based on personal experience I absolutely agree. Because of this truth, I do encourage you to at some point to put a price tag on what you have to offer. However, you must realize that the people on the receiving end ultimately determine the value. Though making a profit is allowed, just remember you should not assume you will make a profit and nor should it be the driving force in you crafting your *why*. Income is always congruent with impact. If you are truly making a difference, financial success will come organically. So focus on your *message* rather than *money*.

Guiding Questions:

- What is your real WHY for seeking to move your life to the next level?

- How will your work serve and impact others?

- What sacrifices are you willing to make to engage in the process of creating a life of purpose? What things are you willing to give up?

"I don't know how I keep going; I just know WHY."
-Coach Ona Brown

Lesson 9 Self-Reflection Notes

_____

_____

_____

_____

_____

_____

_____

_____

_____

_____

_____

_____

_____

_____

_____

_____

_____

_____

_____

_____

_____

_____

Lesson 10

You are what you eat...what goes in must come out!

 A NATURAL process conveys to us the cycle of intake, digestion and output. Think in very simple terms about your diet. Something goes in; it is converted or changed into various forms, and then a release reminiscent to what was consumed takes place. Without going into further detail because of the nature of the example, let's suffice it to say "what goes in will always come out." Just ask my beloved Madison who swallowed a small earring when she was two!

In a world where people are growing more aware about the long-term effects of certain types of food, the need and desire to examine food choices is becoming a very popular one. Countless studies at our disposal outline in great detail the impact consuming certain foods infused with chemicals and preservatives exert on the human body. Though this is not a literal lesson on diet, it certainly is figuratively. Simply put, it is impossible to eat a diet filled with foods of little or minimal nutritional value and expect to look and feel great. If you desire to experience life at its best, great health is at the core. Our health is in most cases naturally linked to what we consume. And so it is when living a life filled with purpose and passion is the goal. You cannot consume disbelief for breakfast, low expectations for lunch, doubt for dinner and expect to produce greatness in your life.

If you are ever are to reach great heights, you must be very selective and intentional about what you take in, because it shapes the very nature of what comes out. You must begin to guard you ear gate and eye gate with extreme caution and diligence. Just as a person who is looking to have a better outward body image by eating better must first change their diet, you too must be willing to look at some of the "comfort foods" that are the cause of your lacking outward performance.

As I transitioned to passionpreneur I became a self-proclaimed student of success. I have always been intrigued by the stories of those who've achieved massive success and were making their mark in the world. I desperately needed to be instructed on how to reach my next level and knew the value in learning from those who had done so. As I opened myself up I became a magnet for information. There were times when I would walk in a bookstore or turn on my computer and gravitate towards titles that embodied the exact pieces that I needed at that very moment to move forward. At every waking moment I was reading a book or listening to teachings and speeches to feed my dream.

Similar to most people, I too had become a reality television junkie. Now with a sense of urgency about my future, I gladly gave up the time I previously spent losing brain cells because working on my dream and preparing for my new reality had become my greatest priority. Please know that I did not share that tidbit as an indictment on reality television. I still enjoy television occasionally on a quiet, rainy afternoon home alone. I just no longer spend an inordinate amount of time watching other people live out a false sense of reality scripted for viewers' entertainment. Creating *my* new reality became more important and actually more fun!

I made a choice to budget my time more responsibly. Choice is one of our greatest assets as human beings and it is always with us. Even before I knew I would write this book I became an avid scribe. I began to carry a notebook with me each day so I could record enlightening thoughts and revelations as I was listening or reading. My car became my center and sanctuary, the place where I could hear and see. I venture to say some people would probably describe me as becoming a bit fanatical in my studies. At the time, I would continue to write without really understanding why. Several months later, when the concept for this book became evident, I played back in my mind the previous months. Those spiral notebooks filled with scratches of inspiration became the lessons I now share with you in this book, hopefully in an effort to help you move forward in life.

It was and still is through that kind of repetition and exposure that I continue to grow and learn. This is the way I developed my voice and found clarity. Most of my key understandings in life appeared once I realized the inherent power in being selective concerning what I was taking in. This is why investing in personal development materials is priceless. Having the right information allowed me to be inspired and ultimately moved me to implementation. When you are fortified with the right information it is hard to be misled. Through allowing new information into my being, new thoughts and beliefs began taking root in me and flowing from my being. In particular, my thought processes and conversation were impacted.

Though making such a change is easy to do, it is even easier *not* to do. This is akin to the person who knows consuming certain foods is counterproductive to their goals but eat those foods anyway. If you are not committed to the process of evolution, it will start but be very short-lived. This is the thinking that makes short-term dieting ineffective! People want the results but are really not willing to make the lifestyle change needed to sustain their weight loss goals. Being a sponge for inspiration and information is now a very integral part of me. This is not something I did long enough to move one step and then stop. The same effort that it took to get to the place I am now will be needed, and even more intensely, to continue to soar. Growing is the very essence of living.

I believe a unique measure of change in "diet" is required for every person looking to make the mental shift necessary for moving to their next level. I was desperate for change so I had to take drastic measures. I would never submit to you that you have to do *exactly* what I did to make your move. I will however, assert that a change *of some sort* is inevitable and should be welcomed. If you don't do away with the trash coming into your life from unproductive sources and replace them with more useful ones, you will never have room for growth. Consider your mind to be a plate you are holding. It can only hold so much at one time. If you are holding a plate filled with items that cannot help you produce your desired outcomes in life, one by one you must remove them from your plate. No one can do this for you. You get to choose when, how, and if the items are ever replaced. Lifestyle changes can take time to become embedded in our normal routine. Be patient with yourself and vow to make small changes daily.

Guiding Questions:

- Who are you listening to and learning from? Are you taking information and getting instructions from credible sources needed to improve your life?

- Make a list of 3-5 "items" you know you must remove from your plate to make room for new ones. What are some barriers you anticipate in doing so?

- What are some practical ways you can seek out and take in the information necessary to provide you inspiration and instruction?

"You're the same today as you'll be in five years except for the people you meet and the books you read."
- Charlie "Tremendous" Jones

Lesson 10 Reflection Notes

_____

_____

_____

_____

_____

_____

_____

_____

_____

_____

_____

_____

_____

_____

_____

_____

_____

_____

_____

_____

_____

_____

_____

_____

_____

_____

_____

_____

_____

_____

_____

_____

_____

_____

_____

_____

_____

_____

_____

_____

_____

Lesson 11

Create SMART Goals to stay on track.

As A former principal I know all too well the role goal-setting plays in building a culture of personal accountability and achieving results. If goal-setting is done holistically, it will span from a macro to micro perspective. Until every person sees themselves and what they do individually as part of the greater good in an organization, let's suffice it to say setting goals can be challenging. We never accomplished anything significant for our students in the absence of clearly defined organizational goals. Written goals were often the thread that held us together and kept us focused in tough times. In the midst of differing opinions and personal agendas, written goals were often used as a consensus-building tool.

At the beginning of each year we would create SMART goals for the entire school and then for individual teachers and staff members aligned to our school mission. Using this criterion is an effective process for setting and achieving your personal and professional goals. This framework to formulate goals has been used for decades by organizations of all types including schools, churches, businesses, and even families. The first-known use of the term SMART goals occurs in the November 1981 issue of *Management Review* by George T. Doran. The acronym was originally outlined as:

- **Specific** – target a specific area for improvement.
- **Measurable** – quantify or at least suggest an indicator of progress.
- **Assignable** – specify who will do it.
- **Realistic** – state what results can realistically be achieved, given available resources.
- **Time-related** – specify when the result(s) can be achieved.

The principal advantage of SMART objectives is that they are easier to understand, to do, and then be reassured that they *have* been done. Over the years the acronym has evolved as goal-setters have adapted and customized them to meet individual needs. There are now several newly accepted criteria as seen below:

Letter	Most Common	Alternative
S	specific	Significant, stretching, simple, sustainable

M	measurable	Motivational, manageable, meaningful
A	achievable	Assignable, attainable, actionable, action-oriented, adjustable, ambitious, aspirational, acceptable, aggressive
R	relevant	Result-based, results-oriented, resourced, resonant, realistic, reasonable
T	time-bound	Time-oriented, time-framed, timed, time-based, time-specific, timetabled, time limited, time/cost limited, trackable, timely, time-sensitive

[1]

Since *you* are ultimately responsible for your results, *you* will be ultimately responsible for ensuring that goals are outlined to help benchmark your progress towards your desired results. Depending on the nature of your goal, any combination of criterion could be used. Below is an example of a thoroughly written SMART goal:

---

[1] http://en.wikipedia.org/wiki/SMART_criteria

Broad Goal: I want to grow my business.

- **Specific:** I will acquire three new clients for my consulting business.
- **Measurable:** I will measure my progress by how many new clients I bring on, while maintaining my current client base.
- **Attainable:** I will ask current clients for referrals: launch a social media marketing campaign and network with local businesses.
- **Relevant:** Adding additional clients to my business will allow me to grow my business and increase my revenue.
- **Time-Based:** I will have three new clients within two months.

SMART Goal: I will acquire three new clients for my consulting business within two months by asking for referrals, launching a social media marketing campaign and networking with local businesses. This will allow me to grow my business and increase my revenue.

Goal setting is a very necessary part of any dream that should not be underestimated in terms of effectiveness. I highly suggest posting your goals in a highly visible place and reciting them frequently throughout the day, even committing them to memory. Use your goals as a compass when you become conflicted or indecisive. Make it a point only to entertain ideas, thoughts and circumstances that will bring you closer to the achievement of your goals. You may realize some part of your goals may be too lofty or too low. If that is the case, know that it is a living document and can be adjusted as needed.

If your goals are to serve as your guide, they must be created with your ultimate desires in mind. Celebrate your successes big and small and vow to learn from your failures. As you continue to grow, commit to outlining your goals and what will be required for achieving success in all that you do.

Here are some things to remember about the importance of writing your goals:

- It becomes a written contract to you which usually <u>sparks a personal motivation</u> to achieve them.
- It makes you define clearly what your goals are. Writing them down encourages you to state what you want in greater detail.
- It frees your mind of perpetually thinking and "remembering" your goals.
- It stimulates creativity and motivates you to think about the next step.

Guiding Questions:

- With no written goals, how will you know what your targets are or when you have accomplished them?

- Have you attempted to set goals in the past and failed to follow through? If yes, explain why.

- Using the sample provided as a guide, set aside the time to write your SMART goals for the next 1-3 months.

"Crystallize your goals. Make a plan for achieving them
and set yourself a deadline. Then, with supreme
confidence, determination and disregard for obstacles
and other people's criticisms carry out your plan."
-Paul Meyer

Lesson 11 Self-Reflection Notes

_____

_____

_____

_____

_____

_____

_____

_____

_____

_____

_____

_____

_____

_____

_____

_____

_____

_____

_____

_____

Lesson 12

Seek to create significance rather than success alone.

 WHILE WRITING this book our world lost a giant in the person of Dr. Myles Munroe, internationally-renowned preacher and transformational leader. I can remember reading the news and experiencing a surreal feeling. Almost immediately social media outlets began to buzz with the details of the deadly crash. I was still high from the synergy created in the room from Gathering of the Giraffes, the women's empowerment network I had just launched.

As I internalized the news of Dr. Monroe's death I thought to myself, there lay a man (along with eight others) who had spent decades compelling others to identify and live in their purpose through his motivational speeches, riveting sermons and infectious personality. Though I mourned the loss with the rest of the world, I also chose to see his passing as an opportunity to self-benchmark. I did not know Dr. Monroe personally, but I knew of his work and had heard him speak in times past. To say he was insightful and impactful is an understatement. I believe that any sane person who dared to explore the depths of his teachings had been changed in some way.

In my reflective nature I asked myself a simple, yet telling question: 'If I had perished in that crash would I have died empty?' At that moment in time the answer was "No." With the dozens of published books, sermons and speeches delivered through the course of his ministry Dr. Monroe definitely left his profound signature in the earth. Without question, the world knew he had been here. Consequently, I fully realized that working to leave a significant mark in the world *had to be* at the forefront for the second half of my life.

Prior to making the leap into passionpreneurship me and my husband's life looked ideal to outsiders looking in. We were both college-educated school principals earning a six-figure salary. We lived in a beautiful home in a cozy middle-class neighborhood. We had managed to create two healthy children to add to the mix. Family vacations and weekend getaways were a part of our norm. If we wanted to buy something, most times we were able to do so. We'd always managed to have money set aside for emergencies. Not to mention we were in good health and enjoyed very fulfilling relationships with our friends and family. We had achieved a level of success together that surpassed anyone else in our families. We were grateful and believed that God had blessed our lives tremendously.

However, at the height of it all we were still hungry for more. We always knew we could not only have more, but more important, do more. When we spoke about expanding our lives people thought we were insane. Why couldn't we just be happy where we were? It definitely would have been much easier. There is nothing easy however involved in any phase of dream- building.

At the time we could not articulate why we felt the way we did. We were no longer interested in just earning a living at the expense of leaving a legacy. We now understood we were being summoned to live a life of significance.

Success can be the enemy of significance. Like many others we had been lured into working harder on our jobs than we were on our dream. The hustle and bustle of going to work, going home, going to bed and doing it again and again on autopilot for the next 30 years was suddenly frightening. We had officially grown tired of living for the weekend. Though education is a noble profession, we believed that we had been called to impact the world. There had to be a way to share our talents and gifts with the world on our terms and create value for other people. If a way didn't exist, we were sure we would create one. We wanted to touch peoples' lives in a way that would leave our signature in the earth. After all, leaving your mark is the only way really to prove you ever lived. Just so you know, your fingerprint on the time clock at your job does not count as your fingerprint in the world - at least in most cases.

Sometimes when you have achieved a certain level of success you can be made to feel guilty about wanting to do more in life. Some will even perceive you as greedy. You may not be struggling financially yet you are still hungry. People at the survival level envy those at the success level. Those who have reached the success level desire to graduate to a level of significance. I submit to you that most people desire to be remembered for doing something great in their world but they end up spending most of their life at "work" and never get around to making a significant difference.

When I think of the life of Dr. Munroe, using his God-given talent to change the world *was* his job. If you are creative, innovative, and determined I believe it is possible to leave a legacy and earn a living at the same time. His life is an exception yet it should be the norm. Please understand, I am not advocating that you abruptly walk away from your job if you find it unfulfilling. I *am* advocating that you find a reason to live and give that has meaning far beyond the name of your employer, your titles or the amount of your paycheck. I know from experience those things are gratifying indicators of success but very often fail in the significance department.

Think of it this way- if you perished unexpectedly tomorrow your employer might (or might not) send flowers in memoriam. Your position might be posted before you were even buried! You'd be missed at the office for a few days until your replacement came on board. Business would resume as usual and your contributions in that work setting would soon be forgotten. This sort of reality check should help you to align your priorities and search for ways to broaden your scope.

Your "dream" is no longer optional but absolutely necessary. Gone are the days of having to choose between having a job or living your dream. You will more than likely have to do both for a period of time. Accept that fact and then let the balancing act begin. Don't be surprised when you feel at times you are living in two worlds at the same time. If your life is ever to have real meaning your top priority must be to get connected and committed to a cause bigger than yourself. If you are truly making an impact, the world will know it and more important, pieces of you will remain in the earth once you've gone. You must begin diligently to build as if your legacy will be determined by each day's end.

Guiding Questions:

- Aside from your family obligations as a spouse, parent, sibling, etc., what is the one thing you desire to do more than anything else in the world?

- If your epitaph was written today how might it read?

- What are three action items you can begin today from right where you are, using what you already have to create more meaning in your life?

"Success is fine, but success is fleeting. Significance is lasting."
- Beth Brooke

Lesson 12 Self-Reflection Notes

_____

_____

_____

_____

_____

_____

_____

_____

_____

_____

_____

_____

_____

_____

_____

_____

_____

_____

_____

_____

_____

_____
_____
_____
_____
_____
_____
_____
_____
_____
_____
_____
_____
_____
_____
_____
_____
_____
_____
_____
_____
_____
_____
_____
_____
_____
_____
_____
_____

Lesson 13

Learn to use the Natural Laws of the Universe to work for you.

I HAD no idea starting out that the universe was so friendly and delighted in bringing into fruition everything I had the capacity to believe and receive. My first experience with understanding universal laws came several years ago after reading *The Secret* by Rhonda Byrne. I was mortified to learn that my thoughts and limited perceptions had actually produced some of the situations in my life that were less than favorable. On the other hand I was relieved and intrigued to learn I had more control than I ever thought possible in terms of shifting my thinking and creating my best life.

As I began to grow in consciousness through personal development I later realized other natural laws existed to assist me in carrying out my heart's desire. Little did I know, because the laws are natural, authentic examples existed all around me. The more I learned, the more I saw. Even when I did not know what terms to use, evidence of these laws appeared in my life. Once I had a better understanding, a new level of living, giving and existing manifested in my life as I was now able to clearly identify and observe the laws at work. My understanding of what happened in my life became less about chance and more about choice. I was able to approach this process of dream-building from a place of power and confidence. Knowing what the "seven laws" are and how they work can make a significant difference in applying them to create the life you truly desire. Below is a brief description of each law.

The 7 Natural Laws of the Universe

The Law of Vibration (The Law of Attraction) states that everything vibrates and nothing rests. Vibrations of the same frequency resonate with each other, so like attracts like energy. Everything is energy, including your thoughts. Consistently focusing on a particular thought or idea attracts its vibrational match. How to apply it: **Focus on what you want instead of what you don't want.**

The Law of Relativity states that nothing is what it is until you relate it to something. Point of view is determined by what the observer is relating to. The nature, value, or quality of something can only be measured in relation to another object. How to apply it: **Practice relating your situation to something worse than yours and you will feel good about where you are.**

The Law of Cause and Effect states that for every action, there is an equal and opposite reaction. Every cause has an effect, and every effect has a cause. Be at cause for what you desire, and you will get the effect. All thought is creative, so be careful what you wish for... you will get it. How to apply it: **Consistently think and act on what you desire to be effective at getting it.**

The Law of Polarity (The Law of Opposites) states that everything has an opposite. Hot-Cold, Light-Dark, Up-Down, Good-Bad. In the absence of that which you are not, that which you are... is not. Polar opposites make existence possible. If what you are not didn't coexist with what you are, then what you are could not be. Therefore, do not condemn or criticize what you are not or what you don't want. How to apply it: **Look for the good in people and situations. What you focus on, you make bigger in your life.**

The Law of Rhythm states that everything has a natural cycle. The tides go in and back out, night follows day, and life regenerates itself. We all have good times and bad times, but nothing stays the same. Change is constant. Knowing that "This too shall pass" is great wisdom about life's ebb and flow. How to apply it: **When you are on a down swing, know that things will get better. Think of the good times that are coming.**

The Law of Gestation (The Law of Gender) states that everything takes time to manifest. All things have a beginning and grow into form as more energy is added to it. Thoughts are like seeds planted in our fertile minds that bloom into our physical experience if we have nourished them. How to apply it: **Stay focused and know that your goals will become reality when the time is right.**

The Law of Transmutation states that energy moves in and out of physical form. Your thoughts are creative energy. The more you focus your thinking on what you desire, the more you harness your creative power to move that energy into results in your life. The Universe organizes itself according to your thoughts. How to apply it: **Put your energy and effort, your thoughts and actions**

into attracting what you desire, and you will surely attract the physical manifestation of that energy.
2

I believe it is imperative to understand that what you don't know *can* and *will* hurt you. If you are oblivious to the fact that universal laws exist, there's no way you can use them fully to produce desired results in your life. Do not continue to move haphazardly through life wishing for luck or some big break that you are not even prepared for. Delve into a personal study of these laws and learn to recognize them at work in your life. The 7 *Natural Laws of the Universe* were created to work *with* you and *for* you. I know from personal experience thoroughly understanding the universe in which we live will be paramount in your moving to the next level. Failing to know and understand the power you have in the process will ultimately impede your progress. Take charge of your life by focusing on what you want, and by law, you will have it.

---

[2] https://gittefalkenberg.wordpress.com/2010/02/28/the-7-natural-laws-of-the-universe/

Guiding Questions:

- What is the universe or what have you thought it to be before now?

- Do you believe the universe plays in a role in your dream becoming a reality? Why or why not.

- What are some ways that you could become more familiar with the universe and the power it holds?

"The universe is constantly saying yes to us. It only says yes. It is our task to discover what within us it is saying yes to." - **Lenedra J. Carrol**

Lesson 13 Self-Reflection Notes

_____

_____

_____

_____

_____

_____

_____

_____

_____

_____

_____

_____

_____

_____

_____

_____

_____

_____

_____

Lesson 14

Take FEAR with you.

It IS perfectly allowable to start your journey with fear in tow. Some of the most incredible moments and memories in my life were celebrated after fear had come and finally gone. Fear can create a range of emotions in each of us including panic, indifference, anger, despair, frustration and worry. Fear can even cloud our thinking and judgment in such a way that we are paralyzed by indecision.

The presence of fear doesn't necessarily mean you are headed in the right direction. It usually means the opposite. You can be on the right path and because you face the unknown, you are fearful. Having reservations and apprehensions about new situations is perfectly normal. Living your dream will be a new experience so feeling a certain level of fear must be expected. However, this is the other side of the fear factor you must ask yourself; "What will become of my life if I *don't* pursue my passion?" You must become more concerned about the consequences of *not moving* as opposed to worrying about any consequences associated with making the shift.

I think back to one of my most dreaded and feared experiences in life: childbirth. From the very beginning my husband and I knew we wanted a family together. After trying for a very short period of time I became pregnant and we were ecstatic! I was even happier to learn that our first child was a girl because this meant I could now overindulge in all the "bling" a baby girl could have. I had just one minor problem - I was afraid of pain. *Very* afraid of pain. Though overjoyed about the impending arrival, I immediately went into stress mode about the delivery. Not to mention all the pricking and prodding I had to deal with from my doctor during the office visits in between. I knew that in order to enjoy motherhood a delivery of some sort was required.

After accepting the inevitable I began to redirect my fear with positive thoughts. Every time I had to go in for blood work I would make a point of remaining positive and upbeat. Every now and again, fear would try to speak. As I prepared for the delivery, rather than overexpose myself to horror stories about childbirth gone bad, I focused on those with desirable endings. I remember the day before my daughter was born my husband and I received a call after a routine weekly checkup. The doctor was concerned that because of my baby's expected size and my advanced age (35 is not advanced by my calculations!) a normal delivery might be too risky. She scheduled birth by C-section for the next day.

Suddenly, I was simultaneously overtaken with excitement and anxiety. Here I was back at this pain issue once more. In that moment I realized and decided I would have to give birth even though I was afraid. I had no other options. I went home and readied the house. The next morning we got up and drove prayerfully to the hospital. I'll spare you the details of what happened over the next few hours- I think you can fill in the blanks. Our daughter was finally born that afternoon and I was relieved from the sense of the unknown that had loomed over me for months.

I was actually surprised at how well everything went with the delivery. Yes, it came with challenges but was not at all the earth-shattering experience I had initially feared. I can remember as a gloating new mom saying to myself later that day 'it wasn't so bad after all.' I even believed since I now knew what to expect, I could find the strength and do it *again*. Two years later I actually did – I gave birth to my son!

Thankfully, I persevered despite feeling afraid. This is the same perseverance I had to call forth to create my best life. The very thought of taking on an assignment that is bigger and more critical than anything else you've ever done in life can be frightening. You will have to do it afraid! Fear is an energy that can be transmuted into another more productive state that will serve you- do not be dismayed. The fearlessness you will need to live your dream can only be wrought from the very same fear with which you started the journey. Not only is this normal, but very necessary.

How can one be an overcomer and they've never been presented with anything to overcome? It will never happen. I believe the presence of healthy fear indicates a dream of such great magnitude, you know a power higher than yourself will be needed to succeed. Fear would be a non-issue if you had it all figured out. Since fear has its birthplace in deception, it can only be conquered by truth. The truth is there is nothing to fear but fear itself! The truth is you have the power to create a life of significance. The truth is there is someone in the earth waiting to meet your dream. The truth is, winning in life is already in your DNA. As you embrace the truth fear becomes obsolete.

So do not lie to yourself or the world and pretend that fear is not affecting you as you pursue your dream. Like anything else in life holding its powers in secrecy, open acknowledgement begins the process of disempowerment. Every time you have fearful thoughts and move forward regardless, fear loses its grip. This is why consistently working despite the presence of fear is so important. As your capacity to defy fear increases, moving toward your dream will become so intense fear will eventually have to find a new home. Fearlessness will set up residency and its opponent is forced to leave. Learning to work past your fears is a cyclical process you will have to engage in each time you grow to a new level. Anyone who has achieved at high levels has at some point experienced a level of fear and you are no different. You can start with fear, but you can't get to new heights with fear at the forefront.

Guiding Questions:

- What do you fear most about pursuing your dream?

- Are you at all fearful about what your life will **not** become if you don't follow your dream?

- Describe in detail what you plan for your life to be in 2-4 years. How might living in fear impact that plan?

"Expose yourself to your deepest fear; after that, fear has no power, and the fear of freedom shrinks and vanishes. You are free." -**Jim Morrison**

Lesson 14 Self-Reflection Notes

Lesson 15

Learn to harness the power of your subconscious mind.

UNDERSTANDING THE role properly utilizing your subconscious mind plays in helping to make your dream a reality is essential. If you can understand the relationship between the conscious and the subconscious minds you will be better able to use them both and at the appropriate times. Somehow, the subconscious is connected to all other minds, and through the Law of Radiation and Attraction it can attract events and people to you that will assist in obtaining you desired results.

One of the first things that you have to understand about your subconscious mind power is that this force is not something imaginary but in reality is an intrinsic characteristic present in yourself even if you cannot realize it. Like other universals truths, your subconscious mind does not stagger in its existence or ability to produce due to your lack of belief or understanding. Actually, the opposite is true. Your being unaware of its power simply means that it is not working on your behalf. In simpler terms, you may be working harder but not smarter on your dreams and goals. Without this key understanding you are probably taking the long way around!

In order to understand fully the power of your subconscious mind you must be able to distinguish clearly between it from your conscious mind. Consider the following:

Conscious Mind vs. Subconscious Mind

- Conscious mind is the part of mind which is fully aware and subconscious mind is a part which is not in complete awareness.
- The information the conscious mind holds is easily accessible but to access information stored in the subconscious mind requires a little more effort.
- Conscious mind is related to actions that are controllable and subconscious mind is related to actions more or less "instinctive."
- Conscious mind is responsible for logic and reasoning but the subconscious mind is responsible for a person's emotions, characteristics, attitudes, desires etc.[3]

It was not until I learned the difference between the two through self-study that I realized I had been feeding the wrong mind, which had hampered my progress in terms of dream-

---

[3] http://www.differencebetween.com/difference-between-conscious-and-vs-subconscious/

building. When you are attempting to live your truth through realizing dreams and working to attain goals, I assure you the path will look and feel unlike anything you've ever known. Your conscious mind because of its emphasis on reasoning, logic, and calculation will immediately deter you. It will recite to you all of the reasons you cannot achieve at high levels, always magnifying limitations.

You will only be lured into your destiny through the feelings and emotions housed in your subconscious mind. This is the place where limitless possibilities constantly fester. In order to live your dream you will need to nurture imagination, inspiration, imagery and intuition. Very little space exists for them in your conscious mind. I now know ignorance caused me to miss so many opportunities in life because I allowed my conscious mind to do all the driving. Ideally speaking, you follow your heart (subconscious mind) but take your head (conscious mind). You will absolutely need both on your journey but knowing when to yield the wheel separates the *dreamers* from *doers*.

I venture to say most people listen to their conscious mind most of the time and rarely allow their subconscious mind an opportunity to speak. This explains the overexposure to comfort zones, limiting beliefs, and unfulfilled lives. You must be willing to take a chance and allow your subconscious mind to lead you. I began to understand my subconscious mind needed to be fortified daily in order for it to guide me on my path. I desired to understand fully its purpose and powers. I constantly read books and listened to teachings on the subconscious mind. With an increased understanding, I was able to quiet the voice of reason every time it prompted me to focus on logic rather than possibilities.

I eventually tuned out everything and anybody that might sway my thinking. I was desperate for change so I became unreasonable in my quest. At some point you must become relentless about your dream. You may even appear a bit high-strung to the ordinary eye and ear. I didn't mind because I understood I had to pay a price for greatness and I was paying my dues. Over time and with much perseverance, I received my breakthrough!

No longer allow your conscious mind to have full control of your future, because it will always have you play small and back down. If you are like most people, you probably have a number of questions concerning how to harness the power of your subconscious mind. I encourage you to do as I did and learn all you can. Understanding the power of the subconscious mind and how to access it will help you to reduce the time it takes for you to reach your goal, whatever it may be. Know that if you continue to do what everyone else is doing, you will only have what everyone else has. Do yourself a favor and do something that you've not done before. Learn how to access the most powerful human faculty given to man-the subconscious mind.

Guiding Questions:

- Are you able to identify the desires and ideas that are present in your subconscious mind? If so, list them. If you cannot identify those desires and ideas, refer back to Lesson 1 to gain clarity.

- Specifically identify the barriers or limitations presented by your conscious mind as you think or act on your desires or ideas.

- Are you fully aware of the power of your subconscious mind? If so, how are you using it create your best life? Explain.

"Whatever we plant in our subconscious mind and nourish with repetition and emotion will one day become a reality." -**Earl Nightingale**

Lesson 15 Self-Reflection Notes

_____

_____

_____

_____

_____

_____

_____

_____

_____

_____

_____

_____

_____

_____

_____

_____

_____

_____

_____

_____

_____

_____

_____

_____

_____

_____

_____

_____

_____

_____

_____

_____

_____

_____

_____

_____

_____

_____

_____

_____

_____

_____

Lesson 16

Frame your world with your words.

So OFTEN when asked a question, before ever calculating the impact of spoken words, most people's responses are filled with affirmations of lack, illness, defeat, misery, mediocrity, and inferiority. Why is this? It appears as if negative talk comes quite naturally yet using positive, uplifting language is foreign and must be contemplated. One form of language serves us and the other does not, yet the one that *does* is harder to speak.

I too have been guilty of unconsciously sabotaging my chances at creating a better life by loosely speaking words and not fully understanding the power they possess. Words are not simply sounds caused by air passing through our larynx. Words have real power. God spoke the world into existence by the power of His word and we are in His image in part because of the power we have with words. Words do more than convey information. The power of our words can actually destroy one's spirit; even stir up hatred and violence. They not only exacerbate wounds but inflict them directly.

Of all the creatures on this planet, only man has the ability to communicate through the spoken word. The power to use words is a unique and powerful gift from God. The idea of our words having power is promulgated in scripture in Proverbs 18:21which reads, *"Death and life are in the power of the tongue, and those who love it will eat its fruit (NKJV)."* Are we using words to build up people or destroy them? Are our words filled with hate or love, bitterness or blessing, complaining or compliments, lust or love, victory or defeat? Like tools, words can be used to help us reach our goals or to send us spiraling into a deep depression. Simply put, we have the power to kill and to create situations in life with our words. Consider these words of famous British author and poet, Rudyard Kipling and you can understand the true power of words: "Words are, of course, the most powerful drug used by mankind."

I believe the words we use are determined by the condition of our heart. We must examine our heart-space to identify the reasons our words are either adding to or robbing us. If you are struggling to think and speak positivity over your dreams and goals, take a look at what's in your heart. If your heart is filled with doubt, fear, jealousy, rage, and greed quite naturally evoking productive words and emotions will be challenging. In order to condition your heart for the journey some "mirror work" is required. Examine closely the feelings you carry about who you are, what you have done or where you have been. Make a point of releasing yourself of all emotional baggage in your past. Accept the things that are out of your control and take possession of the areas in your life you have the power to change. Stay open and know just because something exists doesn't mean it has to remain. Allow your heart to be free and filled with love at all times, even in times of uncertainty. We are advised in this matter in scripture in Proverbs 4:23: *"Keep your heart with all diligence, for out of it spring the issues of life (NKJV)."* Know that every word you speak will reveal what is in your heart.

Finally, I want to caution you against the lasting effects of negative self-talk. We all have a constant stream of thoughts going through our minds. Often the thoughts are about what we don't like about our life. Most times we're not even truly conscious of these thoughts- yet they are creating our future experiences! Consciously practicing making positive affirmations is a way to re-train your mind to think differently and to focus on what you want. Affirmations are positive statements describing a desired situation, event, habit, or goal. When these positive statements are repeated often, mentally or aloud, they are engraved in the subconscious mind. This changes the programming of your subconscious mind, which consequently, transforms the way you think, your habits and attitude, and helps you attract new opportunities and achieve success.

What you think and say about yourself is far more impactful than you might imagine. Too often we focus on what others have to say about us when our goal should be to ensure negative self-talk does not go unchecked. Our thoughts become things, and we get what we think about. Be sure to develop a habit of arresting powerless thoughts, words and images that cast doubt upon your vision. Learn to refute quickly any lies by replacing them with truth and love. Because your inner-self accepts as fact anything repeated frequently and convincingly enough, using positive affirmations will be instrumental to framing with your words the world you desire. You can create positive affirmations for any area of your life you want to improve by using the following principles as taught by Louise Hay, one of the modern pioneers in the use of affirmations to make dramatic changes in your life:

8 Principles for Creating Powerful Affirmations

- *Decide what you want.*
- *Make sure your affirmations are positive, present tense, and personal.*
- *Include words that convey positive, energetic feelings.*
- *Let go of your timeline and trust the timing for delivery.*
- *Let the Universe decide HOW your affirmations will be fulfilled.*
- *Allow your Inner Wisdom to guide you in the right balance between action and allowing.*
- *Believe that you deserve a wonderful life.*
- *Feel gratitude to the Universe for fulfilling your orders in the most miraculous way.*
  [4]

Much of what I have accomplished has been achieved by consistently redirecting my thoughts and understanding the power of positive affirmations. Everything existing in my current world was first called forth with my words. This practice might be new for you, so know it will take some time to master. Be gentle

---

[4] http://www.healyourlifetraining.com/positive-affirmations/

with yourself and vow each day to become better at it than you were the day before. Remember, you have the power to live your dream and your words will either build it or tear it down- the choice is always yours.

Guiding Questions:

- In the past, how has your use of words hampered your vision for your life?

- What are three areas in your life you believe can be improved by using positive affirmations? Using the principles outlined in this chapter, create affirmations for those areas.

- What are some *heart-issues* you need to address to allow more freely positive words to flow from your mouth?

"Maturity is the ability to think, speak and act your feelings within the bounds of dignity. The measure of your maturity is how spiritual you become during the midst of your frustrations." **-Samuel Ullman**

Lesson 16 Self-Reflection Notes

_____

_____

_____

_____

_____

_____

_____

_____

_____

_____

_____

_____

_____

_____

_____

_____

_____

_____

Lesson 17

Change your circle, change your life

I BET you personally know and can list at least five couples that at one time appeared inseparable suddenly announced a split and stated to the world they'd grown apart. I know I can name at least five times that number of couples! I believe what happens in most cases is one person evolves into a higher state of being and the other does not. The person who does not evolve is usually unaware that their refusal to grow, directly or indirectly, will create space in the relationship, making communication and common ground almost impossible. For example, one party is hopeful in creating a future colored with endless possibilities while the other believes their present state is as good as it gets. One person wants to explore news areas of passion but the other doesn't even have the capacity to realize such a thing exists. The list of polarizing mindsets can become endless.

Only one of two things will usually happen when couples reach this state. The person who grows eventually makes a decision to move their life to the next level *sans* the dead weight, literally and figuratively. They are determined to grow at all costs. The other scenario occurs when a person decides it's easier to stay put and not make any waves, relinquishing any thought of a better life. These may be extreme examples yet I hope you understand that you must make some choices in life if you ever intend to pursue your dreams. Please understand, I am not advocating that you divorce your spouse if they are not open to growth! I am merely making a point as to what happens in ALL relationships and partnerships when a shift in consciousness does not happen for both parties involved. Can two walk together, unless they are agreed (Amos 3:3)? It makes me tired just thinking about trying to make progress alone in a disharmonious relationship. I say that walking as well as working to manifest your dreams would be a grueling task without the right people in your life. In order to get to the next level you will definitely have to make some mandatory deletions to your inner circle.

Do not underestimate the impact disempowering relationships can have on your ability to create a better life for yourself. Not having certain people in your life may be frightening to think about but I imagine it would be even scarier if you keep them around. Plainly put, some relationships are parasitic in nature and have no place in your life if you ever intend to soar. As you busy yourself becoming better, attrition will help you with this. As the quality of the goals I set for my life drastically increased I became more selective about how I spent my time. Everything about me changed, especially my conversation. Suddenly people that were not on a similar path in life found me boring; eventually limiting the time we spent together. We became incompatible and grew apart much like the couples in the aforementioned examples in this lesson. This type of natural separation works well because it keeps you from having to announce to the world your intentions, appearing fanatical.

You make a bolder statement by allowing your actions to speak for you which will get the attention of those around you, sometimes making them uncomfortable. When you make a decision to create a better life you say with your actions that where you currently are in life no longer serves you. Those who don't feel compelled to grow with you will eventually be left behind. Anticipating this type of falling away can help to keep you focused when it occurs, instead of taking you on an unending emotional roller-coaster ride leaving you clueless as to why your circle is changing. Ridding yourself of these limiting relationships (friends, relatives, colleagues, etc.) is very necessary. You must be willing to clear the way to make room for real growth to occur in your life.

When you are working to elevate your life do not underestimate the role social capital plays on your journey. Your relationships are often times more critical than money. It's not just about who you know but rather who knows you and what they know about your work. Since God uses people, having the right people in your circle is the only way to move forward. I encourage you to examine thoroughly ALL of your relationships to determine which ones feed you and the life you have envisioned for yourself. Keep in mind that it makes no sense to spend a majority of your time with people who live with limited expectations and expect those relationships to fuel your passion. I personally find that I am most productive and creative when I am in the company of like-minded individuals. Being able to redefine old and create new relationships are both signs that you are a definitely making progress and moving in the right direction. An old cliché states whichever dog is fed the most becomes the strongest. Which dog will you feed? Ask yourself this question daily and remember you always have a choice.

Guiding Questions:

- Are you able to identify at least 3-5 close relationships you have that you know cannot support you in creating your dream? List the names of those people. Examine the reasons you have not ended or redefined those relationships, lessening the impact they have in your life.

- What are some ways that you can forge new relationships and bring people in your life to help build your dream?

- What are some of the reasons you have not been willing to make the hard choices in your relationships required to move your life to the next level?

"I think it happens to everyone as they grow up. You find out who you are and what you want, and then you realize that people you've known forever don't see things the way you do. And so you keep the wonderful memories, but find yourself moving on."
- Nicholas Sparks

Lesson 17 Self-Reflection Notes

_____

_____

_____

_____

_____

_____

_____

_____

_____

_____

_____

_____

_____

_____

_____

_____

_____
_____
_____
_____
_____
_____
_____
_____
_____
_____
_____
_____
_____
_____
_____
_____
_____
_____
_____
_____
_____
_____
_____
_____
_____
_____

Lesson 18

Seek out mentors and coaches willing to show you the way.

IN THE previous lesson I wrote about purposely removing distracting people and relationships from your life. Now that you've started to engage in some relationship purging, you will be able to bring light into your life by removing the dark since the two cannot exist in the same time and space. You will now need to work to replace those unfruitful thoughts and relationships with more productive ones. The Law of Replacement will come into play one you've made this shift. This Law is a truth from the universe which allows you to extract positive energy from a person, place, or thing (thought) from within your atmosphere. You then use the positive thoughts and elements in your atmosphere to replace the negative things you recently extracted. The more negatives you learn to replace with positives, the more positive energy you will invite into your life, thus bringing you one step closer to making your dream a reality.

Negativity appears in your life *unsolicited*; positivity must be *summoned*.

One of the best ways to invite positivity is to seek out coaches and mentors who are engaged in work similar to what you envision for your life. Most people who are fulfilling their purpose are willing to share information needed to help you, and in most cases provide inspiration for your journey as well. You may even know a few already. Don't be afraid to ask them for help. Most truly successful people understand their obligation to light the way for those coming behind them. Their success is often a direct result of helping others. When I decided speaking and writing would be a part of my brand I looked around to see if I knew anyone who could help me. Before having to go too far, I found a couple of mentors within my reach that had done similar work. They were very instrumental in connecting me with resources and other people to move me forward. These mentors were open, honest, transparent, and very secure. They challenged me and guided me in considering facets of my brand that had never crossed my mind. I was able to expand my vision of myself and my talents through rich, scholarly dialogue. Most of what you see in me today is a compilation of experiences and self-revelations gained through meaningful mentoring.

I caution you in this process to only work with people who are willing to openly share with you and believe (shown forth through their behavior) there is room at the top for everyone. The reality is some people will be hesitant to help you if they believe even for a nanosecond you have the capacity to outperform them or if they believe helping you might create competition for them. If you perceive that the people you have sought out as mentors feel more like competitors, don't be afraid to sever ties. If you are discerning, you should detect it. If you encounter this attitude while looking for help, remain focused and know there is someone designated in the earth to help build your dream. Keep looking and keep asking. The only person you should be interested in competing with is you!

If finding someone is a challenge, know that virtual mentoring and coaching can be extremely beneficial too. I've made some substantial progress in my pursuit just by listening and internalizing the teachings of people I've never met face-to-face. Depending on the nature of your dream I would even suggest that you look into hiring a coach to guide you in attaining your desired results. Ask for testimonials from others that have completed their courses before committing.

Though you may find relationships you can benefit from with little to no cost, investing in more structured and results-driven mentoring and coaching programs should be a viable option. These programs can be very costly so do not approach them with a penny-pinching mindset. If you are struggling with the idea of paying for professional coaching consider this- how much will it cost you if you *don't* invest in your dream? All great achievers agree you cannot put a price tag on the possibilities. Not only will you gain valuable information and strategies, you also stand the chance of forging very strategic, impactful, life-long alliances with people that build and believe in you. When pursuing your dreams, having the right people in your life and circle is a priceless commodity.

Guiding Questions:

- Whose voice (other than your own) are you listening to for the purpose of gaining insight towards fulfilling your dream?

- How would you quantify the impact professional mentoring and coaching might have in your life?

- Make a list of people you would like to be trained or mentored by. Do some research, connect with them on social media and learn more about the programs they offer.

"I am not a teacher, but an awakener." - **Robert Frost**

Lesson 18 Self-Reflection Notes

_____

_____

_____

_____

_____

_____

_____

_____

_____

_____

_____

_____

_____

_____

_____

_____

_____

_____

_____

_____

_____

_____
_____
_____
_____
_____
_____
_____
_____
_____
_____
_____
_____
_____
_____
_____
_____
_____
_____
_____
_____
_____
_____
_____
_____
_____
_____

Lesson 19

Choose your personal excellence over perfection.

 HAVE YOU ever been to an event and wondered who booked the bad-singing entertainment? What about saying to yourself on the ride home, "My food is better than that" when you leave a catered event. How about leaving somewhere and saying to yourself, "I thought about doing that?" Well, there's only one difference in you and them: they are moving and you are "thinking" about moving. They didn't wait for the perfect time. They pressed play and used what they had to get started. This is why you have gifted singers who never get booked or superb cooks who never get catering gigs. The person with mediocre talent gets the job because they are in activity mode and the one with an extraordinary gift is parked in contemplation. Although they are both talented, one is *acting* and one is *waiting*.

So instead of waiting on the ideal time, people or circumstances to come about, use what have to debut your dream to the world in your own spirit of excellence. This means that at the moment in time of your debut, your products or services should reflect your absolute best. As you grow, the quality of your work will grow as well. Allow experience to teach you. Establish a system for receiving feedback and use the data to improve your products or services. Become a student of those in your industry doing what you desire to do at an exceptional level. If you commit to the growth process, you will know more in 2 years than you did when you started. You have to be okay with "growing as you go." Doing so will allow you to maintain a sense of pride and integrity about your work at its current level.

Acting instead of waiting is a struggle for most people because they confuse excellence with absolute perfection. The problem with perfection is that it is relative and can be elusive. What happens is most people hold themselves to a ridiculously high standard which keeps them from taking action. They say things like "I'll do it when everything is in place" or "once I find the perfect place." Years pass and they are still waiting. Perfection usually never comes so what often happens is you don't learn how to make *what you have in the moment* work for you. Waiting for perfection is a stall tactic that keeps your dream on hold. The time comes when you must decide to take action *where you are with what you have*. Despise not the days of small beginnings (Zechariah 4:10).

This lesson takes me back to 2014 when I launched my women's network, *Gathering of the Giraffes*. I knew as I was building my dream others would benefit from the like-minded camaraderie the network would provide. Rather than wait until I had achieved all that I desired (which might take years), I understood the "progress in the process" and wanted to share it with other women on their journey. I had in mind what I envisioned the organization to be and I needed to plan a launch event to introduce it officially to the world. Now the question had to be answered, 'how will I pay for it?' This question always has a way of causing people to stop. I was receiving unemployment benefits at the time and things were tight, really tight. Yet, I felt very strongly that the launch was to take place in 2014, not 2015. Waiting would lead to further inactivity, thus stifling my dream. I set a date on the calendar for the launch and announced it the world. I knew stepping out would push me to produce, making retreat almost impossible. With a little creative visioning, bartering, asking, praying and prioritizing, I eventually pulled it off. Every single person that I asked for help obliged. The launch event was amazing and executed with excellence. A group of 30 ladies gathered that day to make the dream of launching *Gathering of the Giraffes* a reality for me and I was thankful.

Don't confuse small beginnings with sloppy beginnings. I believe you have to start where you are, yet always maintaining a standard of personal excellence. For example, you may not have thousands of dollars to invest in advertising but you may have to spend hundreds. Find professionals who can help you market your work at a nominal fee. People eat with their eyes first, so misrepresenting your brand with poorly put together marketing materials might cost you potential clients or customers. First impressions really are lasting.

Be aware of what you don't know and make a decision to invest at a level in alignment with your current resources. In other words if you are not a web-designer, do not try and create your own website. Look for someone who can help you within your price range, or increase your budget if you find out the designers in the lower price ranges don't meet your standard. Remember we tend to experience the greatest amount of frustration when we are operating outside our giftedness. Ask for referrals from others or even barter services to get the job done. Consider sharing your gift with the world in phases rather than all at once. Do what you can in excellence now and work to phase in the rest. *The goal is to take immediate action.* Be creative and innovative- just make sure that whatever you do is done well. Be sure to get advice and feedback from those whose opinion you trust.

Because you only get one chance to debut your dream, doing so in excellence is key. The level at which you present your "stuff" to the world will speak for you before all else. Free yourself from the paralyzing chains of perfection. Every thinking person has the power and the obligation to create a personal standard of excellence from which they work and live. There is a magic alive in this present moment. Use it!

Guiding Questions:

- Which pieces of your dream can you do now? Make a list of resources you have available to you now to get started (people, places, things, ideas, etc.).

- What will it cost you to launch your dream today? Remember, you can roll it out in phases if your resources are limited.

- How much (specific dollar amount) are you willing to invest in getting started *today*? If the amount is not enough, what are some things you could do to generate money to fund your dream?

Stefani McDade Morrow

"I am careful not to confuse excellence with perfection. Excellence I can reach for; perfection is God's business."
-Michael J. Fox

Lesson 19 Self-Reflection Notes

_____

_____

_____

_____

_____

_____

_____

_____

_____

_____

_____

_____

_____

_____

_____

_____

_____

_____

_____

_____

_____

_____

_____

_____

_____

Lesson 20

Use creative visioning to build your desired life.

 A VISION board is a simple yet powerful visualization tool that activates the universal Law of Attraction to begin manifesting your dreams into reality. The concept of the vision board (also known as a goal board, goal map, or treasure map) has been around for generations, but it has gained a renewed popularity in recent years. A vision board is simply a visual representation or collage of the things that you want to have, be, or do in your life. It consists of a poster or foam board with cutout pictures, drawings or writing on it of the things that you want in your life or the things that you want to become. Somehow, the subconscious is connected to all other minds, and through the Laws of Radiation and Attraction your subconscious can attract events and people to you that will assist in the manifestation process. However, your subconscious will only find ways to make the image real if that image is clear and convincing - hence the importance of the mental pictures of success you feed your mind.

It is paramount that your vision board reflects ideally *everything* you desire to be, do, and experience in life.

I can remember making my first vision board with my husband right after we were first married. As I reflect, I can truly say that we always had a bigger vision for our lives. Not fully understanding the power this tool held we set out to collect images and words that spoke to our future. We posted images that showed us making more money, buying a new house, and even having children. Oddly enough we say all the time our children actually look a lot like the cute little faces we placed on that board years ago! We placed our board in our home office and each day caught a glance of our future by taking in those images and words.

I can tell you that every single thing we posted on that board has manifested over the years. Because with time those images became a part of our mental landscape, the circumstances and people emerged in our lives and appeared on the material plane. Seven years later we have grown and so has our vision of ourselves. We still use vision boards to plan for our future and have even started including our kids in the process. My five-year old daughter Madison is fascinated with airplanes and voted to include an image of her on an airplane on the board. Needless to say her very first plane ride will happen later this year!

Though there is no right or wrong way to create a vision board, here are some key understandings that I believe will help to maximize your results:

- Position your board in a place that gives you daily access to multiple exposures if possible. The frequency will help to ingrain the images in your psyche. Anything that your subconscious mind takes in frequently and convincingly enough, it believes and will work to manifest on your behalf.

- Do not allow negative people such as mockers, scoffers, haters, dream-killers, faith-busters, hope-snatchers and the like any access to your vision board. Their skepticism, criticism, and negative energy will interfere with the positive energy you are creating in the atmosphere. Redirecting negative energy will take time and may even cast doubt in your heart, so avoid this pitfall and share your vision board only with like-minded individuals.

- In a sense, your vision board is a living document. This means your board should change as often as you change. As things on the board start to manifest consider removing them and adding new images. As your level of thinking is elevated, update your board. You may find along the way that some of the things that you initially posted aren't as important to you after all. If so, replace them with more significant ones instead. You want your board always to reflect your current state of consciousness so don't emit mixed signals and emotions.

- Do not forget to include images and pictures that reflect you doing the *work* it will take to make the other images (cars, houses, etc.) a reality. In other words, you must envision yourself providing the products or services that will generate the resources required to obtain your heart's desires. For example, my current board reflects images of public speakers, trainers, authors and entrepreneurs engaged in their work. I now see *myself* working in those roles and being handsomely compensated for doing so. The compensation I envision allows me access to the lifestyle outlined on my board (i.e. writing a $50,000 check for a gift or living in my dream home). *Do not make the mistake of creating a board that reflects the lifestyle of the rich and famous but the work ethic of the broke and lazy.* I believe this piece is the most important in the process and yet the most overlooked. Just know that you will have to '*do*' something to get what you want.[5]

Vision boards are a powerful tool that can help you expand your self-perception and explore limitless possibilities. They are inexpensive to make but their potential value to you is immeasurable. Figure out what you want in your life. Next, commit yourself 100% by taking the first step of creating your vision board and activating the Law of Attraction to pull your dreams into reality. Look at the images and words you have

---

[5]

http://www.selfgrowth.com/articles/How_to_Use_a_Vision_Board_to_Activate_the_Law_of_Attraction.html meticulously selected with high levels of intensity and belief each day. Settle on what you see and go to work!

Guiding Questions:

- What is your most deeply held desire in life?

- What is the product or service you see yourself providing that will create financial resources?

- How might using vision boards impact your belief?

"All successful people men and women are big dreamers. They imagine what their future could be, ideal in every respect, and then they work every day toward their distant vision, that goal or purpose." **-Brian Tracy**

Lesson 20 Self-Reflection Notes

_____

_____

_____

_____

_____

_____

_____

_____

_____

_____

_____

_____

_____

_____

_____

_____

_____

_____

_____

_____

Stefani McDade Morrow

_____
_____
_____
_____
_____
_____
_____
_____
_____
_____
_____
_____
_____
_____
_____
_____
_____
_____
_____
_____
_____
_____
_____
_____
_____
_____

Lesson 21

Make it your business to understand the science of believing.

UNTIL RECENTLY, the notion of *believing* was something I thought I understood. Because belief is such huge factor in determining whether or not you reach your full potential, I had to examine closely my own paradigms. I was raised in the church so quite naturally certain teachings were deeply ingrained in my psyche. Belief was one of those teachings in addition to countless others. In terms of belief, the scripture referenced most often was Mark 9:24 which reads, *"If you can believe, all things are possible to him who believes (NKJV)."* I had heard millions of times to just *believe*. In times of desperation, just believe. During periods of hopelessness, just believe. When faced with indecision, just believe. Belief had for years been offered as the solution to any problem that one might face. I believed that my commission was simply to *believe*. However, as I began to grow to new heights in my thought processes, I could not help but reflect on my past belief system. In doing so I had to ask myself, "If all things were possible as a result of my believing, why are my outcomes so disappointing?" There had to be some missing pieces to my belief system because my possibilities had been limited. I absolutely intended to live a life filled with endless possibilities so I had some learning to do.

One of the first things I did was dissect the actual verbiage in the "just believe" scripture (Mark 9:24) at the core of my belief system. Let me insert I do actually believe and seek to live by the truths promulgated in scripture. My dissecting was not to dispute the text, but instead to gain a deeper insight as to why *my* belief had not produced certain realities in my life. Hanging at the very front of the verse is the conjunction "if" which is defined by www.dictionary.com as:

1. [if] conjunction- in case that; granting; or supposing that; on condition that.

The very first realization was that belief is actually conditional, not absolute or automatic. After much study I now understand there will be some who can and others who cannot. Simply put, if I was able to believe then all things were possible for me and if I did not my possibilities were limited. I had never absorbed this truth through that lens. For my entire existence I thought that my belief existed merely because I confessed it. I had no idea that the possibilities were congruent with my level of belief.

My belief should actually be evident in my behavior. If I really believed the sky was the limit, it had not been mirrored in my thoughts or in my actions. To say that you believe and then continue to operate with limiting beliefs is counter-productivity at its highest. I do not blame my spiritual teachers from past. They did not know and had only been able to teach at the level in which they understood. I had been instructed in love (but ultimately in error), "all things are possible" yet my teachers had neglected to explain it was based on the condition that I believe. I set on a path to learn what belief really entailed.

On the subject of belief here are some probing questions I sought answers to:

- How do I *know* I believe?

- What does believing look like?

- What impacts my belief?

- What challenges my ability to believe absolutely?

It was not until I read *The Magic of Believing* by Claude Bristol that I was able to find answers and the missing parts to my belief system. The book's strongest message is simple: virtually anything can be yours, and you can be anything, if you are able to develop a "knowing" about it that you don't ever need to question. Your belief about yourself and your place in the world is inarguably the chief determinant of success.

Belief is the common thread that runs through the lives of those who have achieved at levels inconceivable to the masses. I know this to be true because I have seen it manifested in my own life. When I set out to write this book I started with a very status quo level of belief. I had never written a book but believed my story was worth telling and knew it could be of value to others who were on similar journeys. I knew I *could* do it but was not sure I *would* do it.

I begin to fortify my belief in myself and in my work, only allowing things in my space that would further my cause. I created and used daily affirmations that I repeated until I became convinced. I started to talk about my dream in terms of an expectant child, even setting an arrival date. Every single day *I believed in believing.* And for months, with a gazelle-like focus and with an intensity not previously known to me I finally published my first book. This was the first task that I had completed at what had become my heightened belief level. Something that started as an idea became a reality within a matter of months because I finally understood how to believe.

Thus the startling conclusion: you do not achieve deep felt goals by action alone, but are helped along depending on the quality and intensity of the belief those goals will be achieved. In other words, your belief is determined by what you say - but more important, by what you *do* and how you do it. You cannot move to your next level with a faltering belief system. Know that living a life filled with purpose and passion is possible and do not move from it, in spite of what your present reality dictates.

Regardless of how long it takes or the bumps in the road you encounter on the way, vow to keep your belief in tact. If believing in your dream gets too hard, just hang on to the power of possibility. I can tell you from experience the journey will *challenge* you, but if allowed the chance it will *change* you. Keep in mind that your belief is a natural force and like all others can be used constructively or destructively. Make the choice today to use your belief system to help make your dream a reality.

Guiding Questions:

- What are some ways you can daily engage in belief building?

- How do you *know* that living your dream is possible?

- Identify and list 3-5 barriers to your current belief-system and possible solutions to remove them from your life.

"Believe in love. Believe in magic. Hell, believe in Santa Claus. Believe in others. Believe in yourself. If you don't, who will?" -**Jon Bon Jovi**

Lesson 21 Self-Reflection Notes

_____

_____

_____

_____

_____

_____

_____

_____

_____

_____

_____

_____

_____

_____

_____

_____

_____

_____

_____

_____

Below you will find a list of suggested titles I believe will help you to:
1) expand your self-perceptions,
2) provide clarity in determining your life's work, 3) equip you with
the truths needed to make a mental shift upwards, and 4) eradicate the
limiting beliefs that have kept you from experiencing all that life has to
offer. I hope all of these resources add light to your personal path.

1. Think and Grow Rich *and* Keys to Success: The 17 Principles of Personal Achievement by Napoleon Hill
2. The Millionaire Messenger *and* The Motivation Manifesto by Brendon Burchard
3. The Magic of Believing by Claude Bristol
4. Choosing Your Future by Les Brown
5. The Slight Edge By Jeff Olson
6. Instinct by Bishop T.D. Jakes
7. The Power of Positive Thinking by Dr. Norman Vincent Peale
8. The Strangest Secret by Earl Nightingale
9. The Road to Your Best Stuff by Mike Williams
10. Awaken the Giant Within by Tony Robbins

References

Lesson 1,9
Hill, Napoleon. (1983). *Think and grow rich.* New York: Ballentine Books.

Lesson 11
Doran, G. T. (1981). "There's a S.M.A.R.T. way to write management's goals and objectives". *Management Review* (AMA FORUM) **70** (11): 35–36.

http://sbinformation.about.com/od/startingabusiness/a/smart-goal-examples.htm

http://en.wikipedia.org/wiki/SMART_criteria

http://fitzvillafuerte.com/the-importance-of-writing-down-your-goals-on-paper.html

Lesson 13
https://gittefalkenberg.wordpress.com/2010/02/28/the-7-natural-laws-of-the-universe/

Lesson 15
http://powerofsubconsciousmind.com/
http://powerofsubconsciousmind.com/subconscious-mind-habits/
http://www.differencebetween.com/difference-between-conscious-and-vs-subconscious/

Lesson 15, 20, 21
http://www.butler-bowdon.com/the-magic-of-believing

Lesson 16
Proverbs 18:21 and 4:23 (New King James Version)
http://www.gotquestions.org/power-of-words.html#ixzz3L98ccjzr
http://www.successconsciousness.com/books/affirmations_words_power.htm
http://www.healyourlifetraining.com/positive-affirmations/

Lesson 17
Amos 3:3 (New King James Version)

Lesson 18
http://mastermindarticles.wordpress.com/category/the-law-of-replacement/

Lesson 20
http://www.selfgrowth.com/articles/How_to_Use_a_Vision_Board_to_Activate_the_Law_of_Attraction.html

Lesson 21-
Mark 9:24 (New King James Version)
www.dictionary.com
Bristol, Claude. (1991). *The magic of believing*. New York: Pocket Books.

School is always in session with me...
Let's connect on Social Media!

https://www.facebook.com/pages/FromthePrincipalsDesk2015

https://www.facebook.com/pages/VillaMorrow

https://Twitter.com/Stefani_Morrow

stefanimorrow

Mailing Address
Villa Morrow Empowerment Group
P.O. Box 1581
Midlothian, Texas 76065
www.villamorrow.com

General Information:villamorrow@gmail.com
Booking Inquiries:bookstefaninow@gmail.com
www.stefanimorrow.com

Made in the USA
Middletown, DE
11 August 2015